BAREFOOT DISCIPLE

Barefoot Disciple

Walking the Way of Passionate Humility

THE ARCHBISHOP OF CANTERBURY'S
LENT BOOK 2011

STEPHEN CHERRY

continuum

Published by the Continuum International Publishing Group
The Tower Building, 11 York Road, London SE1 7NX
80 Maiden Lane, Suite 704, New York NY 10038

www.continuumbooks.com

First published 2011

British Library Cataloguing-in-Publication Data
A catalogue record for this book is available from the British Library.

ISBN 978-1441-18286-9

Designed and typeset by Kenneth Burnley, Wirral, Cheshire
Printed and bound by Replika Press PVT Ltd

. . . walk humbly with your God.

(Micah 6.8)

For Bill and Marie, with deep gratitude and love.

Contents

Foreword

The Archbishop of Canterbury

If it's true that humility is necessarily something that happens in you when you're not looking, how on earth do we think about it, let alone make the sort of decisions that might help us grow into it? Stephen Cherry's book is a gently effective clearing of the ground. He guides us carefully through the minefields of definition – positive and negative varieties of pride, humility and the varieties of humiliation, humility and modesty, false and true . . . And above all, he clarifies the intensely *creative* character of humility when it is, in his terms, 'passionate', that is bravely self-confident because self-forgetting.

Humility indeed happens when we're not looking. And that means that we have to learn where to look if we want to grow into the truth. We must look into the purpose, the mission, of God and allow ourselves to be taken up into the terror and exhilaration of this mystery so that we forget to protect ourselves. This is the heart of that childlikeness which Stephen identifies with real Christian maturity. But the opportunity for this does not come only in the context of prayer and praise; it develops in moments when I find I have become a stranger to myself, moments when I have lost my bearings and can't see the way forward – the moments when I have to learn something new in order to live. Wisdom, Stephen writes, 'demands that we take the risk of being overwhelmed'. And this vulnerable willingness to become a stranger and lose our bearings is the key to entry into the world of Jesus Christ: we find ourselves guests of Christ, strangers welcomed into a home, and so learn to exercise hospitality ourselves. In all this too, we come to understand ourselves more fully as bodily beings, constantly tempted to fantasize ourselves out of the material world and to create boundaries between soul and flesh: humility is, of course, incarnation, recognizing that it is precisely as changing and decaying physical agents that we engage with the real world, not the imagined one that we can manipulate for our satisfaction.

Stephen Cherry spells this out with a wealth of often moving personal testimony drawn from encounters with church and culture in many contexts across the world. He writes with transparent clarity and directness, urging his readers to 'choose life' by immersing themselves in the vision of God's transforming purpose, so that they are moved to take off their shoes, instinctively and unselfconsciously, in recognition of a holy love that draws them away from themselves and their private fictions. This is about humility as the deepest kind of realism. It will resonate profoundly with all who are hungry for truth and eager to serve the truth, and I commend it gratefully.

+ Rowan Cantuar:
Lambeth Palace, Michaelmas 2010

CHAPTER 1

Christlike Wisdom

Early one morning I awoke with a start. I was just home from a conference and my head was spinning with ideas. It was 3 a.m. and I was wide awake. Not sure quite what to do, I went to another room and sat at a desk to write down my thoughts. After a while I became sleepy and, on my way back to bed, I decided to get some water from the bathroom. The lights were off. I pushed open a door and stepped forward. Life slowed down as I realized that I was putting my foot not onto the floor, but into open space. 'I can't remember there being a step down into the bathroom', I thought, as I toppled helplessly and irretrievably forward, realizing now that I was falling down the long, steep, dark staircase of the nineteenth-century rectory where I live. As I fell, I remembered stories of people surviving falls because they were so intoxicated that they relaxed. Stone cold sober, I intentionally relaxed into the fall as I bashed into the stairs and the walls on this rapid descent which seemed to last an eternity. Eventually I came to rest, upside-down, among the groceries stored at the foot of this usually unused back staircase. I could not see a thing. It was pitch black, and I was extremely disoriented. After a pause to catch my breath and collect some of my senses, I had no choice but to shout to summon help from the slumbering household. It came in the form of my disconcerted wife. As she helped me to my feet we noticed that a carton of

1

apple juice cushioned my neck and we decided that no bones were broken. I struggled to gain some dignity. In the hours that followed, I both gave thanks that I had not done any serious damage, and also reflected at length, and in increasing discomfort as the bruises began to rise, on the significance of all this. Words from a conversation with an Australian priest about a curate whom he had found particularly trying came back to my mind. 'I kept saying to him, "Get this word into your head, mate: *humility*".' And that is how this book was born. It is an attempt to get the word 'humility' not only into my head but also my heart and bones.

But how is it to be done? Indeed, can it be done? Can we learn humility? If so, what are the resources that might help us to do so? J. M. Barrie said that life is a long lesson in humility, and he may well be right. But we need more than experience alone to help us learn humility. What are the lessons? Who are the teachers? What methods might help? This book is an exploration of these questions. Humility is one of the virtues that lies deep, often hidden, within the character. It makes itself known not in grand gestures, but across the whole of our life. How does it get there?

In this book we consider a wide variety of situations and ask whether reflection on them might help get humility into our heads, hearts and bones. We also do some work to clarify what we mean, and do not mean, when we use the word 'humility', and chart some of the territory where it is found by exploring ideas like pride, humiliation, modesty and wisdom. But we won't get very far with humility if we rely only on ideas. Stories from travel fill these pages, as do reflections on subjects like walking and washing, ageing and grumbling, praying and singing, being generous and, ultimately, being mortal. Most importantly perhaps, we will seek to find a form of humility which is robust and confident enough to cope with the world today and which is true to the example and teaching of Jesus. That is, humility which combines a certain kind of acceptance of vulnerability and suffering with a deep desire and profound determination for the kingdom of God. We will call this *passionate humility* and, as the book progresses, it will be this form of humility that we seek to both understand and absorb.

A Rare and Unfashionable Virtue

Today humility is seriously out of fashion. It is impossibly uncool. So much so that you could say that ours is a humility-averse society. In a dictionary article about humility the author writes that, 'In contemporary Western cultures . . . humility has been marginalised.'[1] There is nothing new in this. Alastair Mac-Intyre reminds us that '[The] only place in Aristotle's account of the virtues where anything like humility is mentioned, it is as a vice . . .'[2] That view is alive and well today. Talk of humility generates hostility. It is as if we are allergic to the word 'humility'. I have noticed that people find it difficult to comment straightforwardly when I have preached about a saint who has a reputation for humility. Chad of Lindisfarne and Lichfield is reputed to have been very humble because, like Aidan, he preferred to walk than to ride a horse. It gave him a better opportunity to meet people face-to-face and eye-to-eye. Listening to other preachers, I have noticed that while they are happy to celebrate such humility, they are reluctant to suggest that people might aspire to humility, though they might be quite unabashed in encouraging people to be wise, generous or courageous. They know it is a risky business. Should a sermon touch on the virtue of humility, you can quickly begin to feel the discomfort. Is the preacher advertising himself as a humble person? How arrogant! Is the preacher advocating that others should be more humble? How oppressive! There is real irony in this; humility is seen as both too modest and too holy to aim at.

And yet, the French philosopher, atheist and author of a best-selling book on the virtues, André Comte-Sponville, rates humility as a 'great virtue', ranking it eighth in his list of eighteen.[3] That is quite astonishing and a sign that values are changing in the twenty-first century. Looking back a few decades, however, we find the agnostic writer Iris Murdoch concluding her famous essay *The Sovereignty of Good* with the belief that humility is, in fact, the central virtue, preferring it to her other possible candidates: love, freedom and courage. In her view, it is humility that has the capacity to integrate other virtues and qualities and, as such, it is the 'sovereign good'. And yet it is underestimated and uncommon.

Humility is a rare virtue and an unfashionable one which is often hard to discern. Only rarely does one meet somebody in whom it positively shines, in whom one apprehends with amazement the absence of the anxious avaricious tentacles of the self.[4]

In his book *Virtue Reborn*, Tom Wright points out that humility, like charity, patience and chastity, are 'commonly recognised as Christian innovations'.[5] However, it is remarkable how little attention we give these virtues today. Might this be partly because we do not believe that they can equip us to cope with the demands of everyday life? Strength, independence, persuasive power and, above all, fame or celebrity, are far nearer the top of the list of values that infuse the public imagination today. We have drunk too deeply the well of the great nineteenth-century masters of suspicion, such as Friedrich Nietzsche, who despised the Christian virtues, believing them responsible for a slave mentality which was, in his view, far too accepting and servile. This, coupled with Sigmund Freud's analysis that we do not know the workings of our own mind but are driven by subconscious forces, means we think that those who aspire to humility are either pathetic or deluded. Either they have lost the guts to try to make a difference or have forgotten how to relish the joys of life. The only other possibility we willingly entertain is that they are trying to dupe us – having first duped themselves. We might even, following Karl Marx, the third grand master of distrust, suppose that they are playing a complex game to protect their own interests.

All this makes humility an extraordinarily difficult subject to get to grips with. We may not have read a word of Marx, Nietzsche and Freud, but their ideas buzz around our heads and undermine not only our innocence, but also our faith. We are very knowing these days. We believe that nothing is quite what it seems. Obsessed with appearance, image and superficiality, we believe that there can be no deep integrity in others, that any apparent authenticity is a sham. Charles Dickens' character Uriah Heap tells us all we need to know about those who claim to be humble. We see through the mask of humility to the ugly face of true guile.

We know that to claim to be humble is to risk being thought of as conceited and boastful, but we also know that it is far more complex than that. All this makes us very self-conscious about it, which is deeply ironic because, as we shall see, humility is the virtue which encourages self-forgetfulness. Nonetheless, just about every book I have read on the subject begins with a word of self-excuse. C. J. Mahaney, for instance, writing from the American Baptist context, says that,

> I could entertain you for hours relating the comments and facial expressions of those who discovered that I was authoring

a work with this title. I can understand their reaction. If I met someone presuming to have something to say about humility, automatically I'd think him unqualified to speak on the subject.[6]

Even in the Church, where humility is foremost among the distinctive virtues, it makes us both dubious and bashful. Perhaps this is why there are relatively few books on the subject to help us. Topics like 'leadership' are far more popular and much less prone to provoking irony or suspicion, even when qualified with words like 'servant'. This seems odd to me because leadership writing is clearly intended to help people increase their personal power and influence. But we do not trouble ourselves when people write, read or teach about leadership in anything like the way we do if they try to engage with humility. Maybe it is because we are on the alert for any tips that might one day give us the edge, the advantage. Humility will never do that. Like the other Christian virtues, there is no reward for humility because humility is not a performance or an achievement. It is, however, integral to the path we have chosen to follow. There is no humility-free form of Christian discipleship. That does not mean that there is no joy in humility. It means that joy and humility are bound up together far more closely than achievement and reward. We will reflect further on this in Chapter 5 where we consider the childlike capacity to delight in things.

Leadership so fascinates us today because it combines two contemporary compulsions: power and celebrity. What an intoxicating combination! No wonder there are countless shelves of books and endless programmes which offer to help us become better leaders, more powerful in our influence over others. Alongside them, and in equal volume, sit the products to help us become either more successful or happier, or perhaps both.

All this stuff engages the contemporary imagination and captures its ambition. Meanwhile, the followers of Jesus of Nazareth are very reluctant to be seen to be thinking that humility is, after all, a very good thing, a central virtue. I say this not with blame but with sympathy. It really is difficult to get our heads round humility and to allow it to sink into our hearts and bones. However, the reality is that there is no alternative. Leadership, success, wealth and happiness are not the right words, the right virtues, for the people of God, the community who seek the kingdom which Jesus prefigured, inaugurated and announced.

One of the great things about thinking in terms of virtues, and Tom Wright brings this out very strongly, is that it is a way of living that orients itself to a goal. The goal of Christian living is to follow Jesus and to share with the other disciples in seeking the kingdom of God. The witness of the New Testament is that this requires distinctive virtues which we have already noted: patience, charity, chastity and, above all else, humility. Humility is not an option for a few who like that sort of thing. It is not a mark of the sanctity of some – though the sanctified will have it in spades. It is not a mere by-product of exceptional discipleship. Humility is central and of the essence; indeed humility is, in the context of the new values and new life of God's kingdom, both strength and integrity of character. Until we get passionate about it we will fail to understand what it was that Jesus was saying, and why his message was so unacceptable then and remains so unpalatable now.

I am passionately convinced that humility is not only a real virtue, both 'great' in Comte-Sponville's terms and 'sovereign' in Iris Murdoch's, but a central and absolutely down-to-earth one which is always both relevant *and* unpopular. However, I feel no need to try to persuade you that I am a humble person, nor, with mannered modesty, to assure you that I am not. Such judgements really do not matter. What matters is embarking on the quest of learning humility, for that is, like it or not, what God teaches us as we follow in the footsteps of Jesus Christ and seek God's kingdom. Success, leadership, fame and happiness might all be by-products of this pursuit. But it is more likely to go the other way. We might well end up, in the world's eyes, at least, unknown and unhappy with no one following us. We are following the one who ended up on the cross, after all.

Learning Humility

Among the many books which promise to teach us how to be successful, one has the paradoxical title *Failing Forward*.[7] It offers the simple, accessible message that, 'the difference between achievers and average people is their perception of and response to failure'. The writer's key point is that 'achievers' do not take a failure as a moral judgement on themselves. They see it as merely a passing event, a transitory setback. They do not interpret the experience of failure as evidence that they are themselves a failure. The logic of this, once you think about it, is alarmingly obvious. You can only win a race if you are one of those to reach the finishing line. You can only achieve after a setback if you have another go. Achievers are, by definition, those who do not give up. No one learns to walk who does not learn how to try again after falling over. It seems odd that a book based on such a simple point should sell millions of copies. But it has. This should perhaps tell us just how strong the tendency is for people to respond to a setback or disappointment in such a way as prevents them persisting. It might sound perverse to connect this with humility, but oddly it is precisely those with a humble attitude who will not be as damaged by failure as those arrogant enough to believe that they should expect to be successful at the first attempt.

'Pride comes before a fall' is a modern saying based on Proverbs 16.18: 'Pride goes before destruction, and a haughty spirit before a fall'. It is an intriguing phrase, taken to mean that if we think or act above our station, if pride takes us over, then it won't be long before something brings us back down to earth with a bump. There is an intuitive truth in this, as I discovered trying to walk around the house in the dark. If we try to achieve a task while we lack the skills or resources that are necessary, then the chances of failure are high and we can end up being humiliated. It is neither wise nor humble to overreach our grasp. Jesus reminds us of this when he tells the story about the man who built a tower without properly calculating the cost (Luke 14.28–30), and follows it up with a parallel one about a king reviewing his resources in the light of those of his enemy before deciding his strategy (Luke 14.31–2). This is why humility is so important in the project of following Jesus and seeking the kingdom of God. Try doing it without humility and you will not only fall at the first hurdle (you will do that anyway), but you will not be able to get up and have another go. That's the power of humility. It does not prevent the fall but it allows us to try again and again and again . . .

In an intriguing passage in Matthew's Gospel, Jesus invites people to come to him for release and comfort.

Come to me, all you that are weary and are carrying heavy burdens, and I will give you rest. Take my yoke upon you, and learn from me; for I am gentle and humble in heart, and you will find rest for your souls. For my yoke is easy, and my burden is light. (Matthew 11.28–30)

This passage follows on from one where Jesus prays with thanksgiving because his Father has 'hidden these things from the wise and intelligent, and revealed them to infants' (Matthew 11.25). Jesus is initiating a new form of understanding and new form of wisdom; we might even call it anti-wisdom. It is not the savvy that we gain with age. Rather it is an 'understanding' which is somehow revealed to infants. It is a wisdom which is intuitive and childlike and which has something very simple, unaffected and direct about it. What it is not is 'common sense'. It is *Christlike wisdom*; the down-to-earth wisdom of humility which itself stands, almost unnoticed, at the heart of this brief passage. It is connected with gentleness, another New Testament trait that is somewhat out of fashion and favour today: 'Take my yoke upon you, and learn from me; for I am gentle and humble in heart . . .' The yoke, the burden, is that of being Christlike. It involves following, but that following is not so much about trotting along some distance behind Jesus, as about emulating his *way* of travelling.

But is it possible to learn humility? The psychologist Everitt Worthington is not sure. 'Humility, if pursued intentionally, is difficult. It requires negating the negative, seeing the self in true perspective, being modest, and pursuing noble purpose.'[8] I do not think Worthington is quite right here, though he does have a good point. While we might think of *acquiring* wisdom or courage, it does not feel right to speak of 'acquiring humility'. The word 'acquire' belongs to the wrong register for the growth in personal humility. The word 'develop' or 'learn' might be better, though neither entirely resolves the tension. There are logical, psychological and spiritual snares at every step. Ironically, the greatest danger for those who make humility their project is pride. Humility is the opposite of pride, and yet, if we value humility and aspire to it, there is danger that, perceiving ourselves to have made a little progress, we might congratulate ourselves and let pride raise its spoiling head. Comte-Sponville opens his essay on humility with the nice irony that, '[Humility] is a humble virtue . . . to pride oneself on one's own humility is to lack it'.[9]

Suppose someone devised a questionnaire to measure our personal humility. And now suppose that you take it and get a low score one year but two years later you take it again and get a much higher score. An improved score on a humility test would be quite difficult to live with. Should we be proud of our improvement? Could we tell anyone about our improved humility score? The thought of boasting of our humility, or advertising it in any way is, depending on your personal taste, either amusing or pathetic. Yet while it is wrong to think that we can make ourselves humble, and morally ridiculous to mark down our humility as an achievement to our credit, I want to suggest that it is right and good to *aspire* to humility. Personal humility is a necessary component of any Christian value system, and so we should seek to learn and develop it.

The effort involved in learning humility, however, is unlike that involved in seeking to fulfil most other aspirations that we might have. Learning humility is not like learning a language such as French, or a skill like riding a bicycle, nor is it like mastering quantum physics or acquiring what London cabbies call 'The Knowledge'. Not only is it far more important, it has different results. Learning humility involves learning at the level that causes us to adjust our sense of who we are and what the world is really like.

We cannot become humble by dint of effort but we can, as it were, 'opt' for a way of living that might lead us in the direction of becoming more humble. This is all of a piece because humility is a component, if not the foundation, of what we might call Christian maturity. And it is also a component, if not the foundation, of Christian friendship. Moreover, it is a component, if not the foundation, of Christian learning. Christian learning is of the essence of what we rightly call discipleship. There is something circular here: we need humility in order to be able to learn, yet one of the things that we need to learn is humility. We return to this puzzle repeatedly, but let us for now note that this means that we will need to start this intentional learning process fully aware that we have a very long way to go and that the journey will proceed slowly. Like a pilgrimage it will go step by step, with some miles feeling much longer than others.

Apprentices

The word 'discipleship' is increasingly used to describe the practice of Christian faith. The idea is that, although the word 'disciples' naturally calls to mind Peter, James, John and the rest of the twelve whom Jesus called to be his followers, the word can be extended to include Christian people today. The disciples are not *them*, or at least not exclusively them, but *us*, all of us who are trying, and who have tried down the ages, to follow the way of Jesus. Based on the Latin word '*discipulus*', which means 'pupil' or 'student', the words 'disciple' and 'discipleship' carry the often hidden message that the quest for authentic, positive, Christian living involves *learning*. Discipleship learning is neither academic nor functional. God's curriculum, if we can think of it that way, is less about learning new things and more about becoming new people. It is not about ensuring that people are being *informed* so much as *transformed*.

One way of encapsulating the tenor of discipleship learning is to think of disciples as Jesus' *apprentices*. Apprentices learn by spending enough time with the master to absorb not only message and method but also wisdom. In the case of Jesus, this wisdom was remarkably practical and down-to-earth. It was expressed in the language of the common people. After all, Jesus himself did not learn by attending an academy. He learnt in a carpenter's shop and at his mother's knee. He was formed by talking with people wherever he met them and by wrestling with demons in the wilderness. Jesus did not teach a course or found a college. Jesus' educational method, as befits one who called himself 'the way, the truth and the life', was to take his disciples with him on his eventful journeys.

True disciples are those who absorb Jesus' wisdom by becoming his travelling companions on the way. What happens to us on the road is a vital source of deep learning and real insight. The journey of discipleship involves crossing the boundaries of our personal comfort zone again and again. This is always going to be disconcerting, and sometimes painful, but it seems to be the way in which God organizes our apprenticeship in Christ. We are true disciples when we are doing our best to latch on to Jesus' way of life by being open to the adventures that God has given us. It is when we take three things together: learning from Scripture, learning from Christ's travelling companions, and learning from our own experience on the journey, that we open ourselves to being constantly renewed. This is what is involved in the adventure of following the Christlike way as down-to-earth disciples.

Discipleship involves learning in a way that is so everyday and ordinary that it is easily overlooked. It is the kind of learning that happens when people are challenged at a deep level and know that they need to think differently to understand, accept and live with the experience. This is the gracious, often relational, learning that changes lives. This kind of learning is not an achievement of the self so much as a forming of the self; a formation of the self into something both more realistic and more holy. Such is discipleship learning and such is the process of growing in humility. The word 'formation' rightly suggests that it has a physical, bodily dimension. When we learn life's most important lessons we are often aware of a profoundly *bodily* aspect to it. Experiences such as bereavement, visiting a developing country, falling in love, caring for a loved one or nurturing a child, all impact on us in this deep, holistic sort of way. They form us. It is such experiences that have made us the person we are today. Christian formation, like humility itself, is a holistic experience and impacts on our attitudes and emotions, our character as a whole.

The Right Kind of Effort

As we have seen, the psychologist Everitt Worthington believes that it is difficult, if not impossible, to acquire humility intentionally. In a beautiful image, he shows how counter-productive it might be to strive after humility, to make the wrong kind of effort or to try to capture it.

> Being humble, then, is like trying to catch air in our hands. The faster we close our fingers around it, the faster the air spurts away. The slower that we close our hands, the slower the air spurts away. But if we hold our hands, palms up, arms outstretched, then air will come to rest in our hands. To experience humility, then, is not to grasp or strive towards it, but to rest as we seek to bless others. When we are moved from within, a humble spirit can descend upon us like that air resting in the open hand.[10]

It is a beautiful and telling image with much to teach us about the acceptance, patience and imagination that are integral to developing humility, and which are all present in the person who has become truly humble. We will need to bear this in mind as we reflect on the kinds of activities, experiences and processes that might help us learn humility and grow in Christlikeness. For growth in humility does not come through a kind of sanctified self-help programme. Rather it comes from the realization that in the deepest, most important and fundamental matters we do not have the capacity to sort ourselves out. Growth in humility happens through a process not of instruction or education as such, but through openness and vulnerability. That is to say, it is grace that makes us humble. Our humility, if it exists at all, is nothing less than the grace of God in us. Does this mean that it is wrong to aspire to humility? Everitt Worthington thinks it is.

Aspiring to humility is forcing the hand closed and clenching the fist. Aspiring to achieve humility is King Kong with his fists clenched, beating his chest, bellowing and calling attention to himself.[11]

But this is perhaps where we need to part company with Worthington and suggest that aspiring to be humble, when humility is properly understood, does not involve drawing attention to ourselves. However, the warning that he gives through the image of the breast-beating, attention-seeking gorilla, while mistaken, is apposite. The image does not speak to us of either humility or pride but of rage. A contemporary reading of *King Kong* would surely emphasize the unjust captivity and the intolerable stress of the noble beast. Indeed, with what we know today of gorilla behaviour we might suggest that King Kong was acting out of character and, had human beings historically exhibited a more humble attitude towards other animals, there might be less scope to use them as images of our own worst features. True humility must allow for the possibility of anger and other strong feelings and also allow us to relate better to God's creatures, indeed the whole of creation. We will explore these issues in Chapters 6 and 9.

Worthington suggests that we can learn more about humility by turning our gaze outwards, than through introspection. He helpfully invites his readers to reflect on people that they know and to identify some 'heroes of humility'. It is worth doing for yourself, and Worthington sets an example by writing about his mother-in-law, Rena Canipe. In her old age Rena struggled with dementia. It is a moving and encouraging story which shows us how a virtue built up over the years becomes a strength in unexpected circumstances. Rena's humility was formed by the way in which she gave herself selflessly in love and service to others, most significantly as a voluntary charity worker with the homeless and with children. This outward-looking love made a difference to other people's lives, but also helped to shape her as a person of genuine and strong humility. Watching his mother-in-law struggle with dementia was a profound experience for Worthington, but he is not romantic about it. For instance, he is determined to point out that while Rena's humility shone through her dementia, that condition was also deeply humiliating. (The relationship between humiliation and humility is important and we will return to it in Chapter 4.) Worthington's account of his mother-in-law suggests that it is not that humiliating experiences make us humble, but that humility can help us cope with humiliation. The effect of humiliation is all too often to poison our sense of who we are, and undermine any nascent confidence. Confidence and humility, on the other hand, can be complementary qualities.

While I believe that it is good for us to try to learn humility, I suspect that most genuine growth in humility is not sought. Rather we find it coming to meet us as we discover that our preferred way (the way of self-confidence, self-achievement, self-justification, self-admiration, self-consciousness, in fact *self-everything*) starts to go wrong. Most people will be spared a tumble down a long staircase, but they will experience something like it. That is, they will not seek the lowest place but they will find the lowest place coming to meet them with a wallop. When you think about it, it is the laws of nature that do this to us most readily: the gravity which sucks us down to earth, the passage of time that erodes our good looks and intellectual agility, the sheer diversity of humanity and creation that gives us so much to wonder and ponder that we end up bewildered half the time. To aspire to humility is to discover what the true meaning of our place in life, in God's creation and providence, might be. More significantly, however, we are turned away from anxious concern about 'our place in things' (distracting self-awareness) to contemplate the things themselves. Isabel Dalhousie, the philosopher heroine in Alexander McCall Smith's *The Right Attitude to Rain*, experiences just this insight as she stares into space:

> She looked heavenwards, and felt dizzied, as she always did when she looked up into an empty sky; the eye looked for something, some finite point to alight upon, and saw nothing. It might make one dizzy, she told herself, but it might make one humble too. Our human pretentions, our sense that we were what mattered: all this was put in its proper place by simply looking up at the sky and realising how very tiny and insignificant we were.[12]

That sense of insignificance is not in itself humility but it is a necessary step on the way. More than that, it is a constant on the journey. When we perceive its majesty, reality itself can shrink our sense of who we are as close to vanishing point as our imagination will go: to the point of infinite insignificance we might say. We need to live with that, to carry that. Not so that we get stuck in it but so that we can begin to discipline our eye to look outward and open our hearts to the love that we can receive from others, the wonder that comes from contemplating the complexity of creation and, in and through and beyond all this, getting a glimpse of the grace that comes from God.

To aspire to humility is paradoxical to the point of being contradictory, counter-cultural to the point of being laughable, and difficult to the point of being impossible. Put this way, we can perhaps see why it lies at the heart of Christian discipleship and therefore Christian learning. The pursuit of humility sets us off on a journey as strange and unfashionable today as Jesus' mission proved to be in his day. There is glory in it; but not the sort the world seeks. There is wisdom in it; but not the sort the world knows. There is learning it; but not the sort the world esteems. Aspiring to humility is, of course, an impossible dream to realize. But it is not a vain dream. Rather, it is the dream that our own vanity will end.

Notes

1. Dreyer, 'Humility', p. 349.
2. MacIntyre, *After Virtue*, p. 177.
3. Comte-Sponville, *A Small Treatise on the Great Virtues*.
4. Murdoch, *The Sovereignty of Good*, p. 103.
5. Wright, *Virtue Reborn*, p. 114.
6. Mahaney, *Humility*, p. 13.
7. Maxwell, *Failing Forward*.
8. Worthington, *Humility*, p. 70.
9. Comte-Sponville, *A Small Treatise on the Great Virtues*, p. 140.
10. Worthington, *Humility*, p. 103.
11. Worthington, *Humility*, p. 103.
12. McCall Smith, *The Right Attitude to Rain*, p. 164.

CHAPTER 2

Learning to Walk

The Plodge

For over 300 years in the Middle Ages, Christian learning for mission prospered in the community formed by Saint Aidan on the Holy Island of Lindisfarne in north-east England. People still make the pilgrimage to this tidal island. In my student days I was able to participate in the ecumenical 'Northern Cross' pilgrimage one Holy Week. Groups of young adults walked from starting points in Edinburgh, Carlisle and, in my case, Newcastle. Between us we carried a large wooden cross, sharing its burden. All the groups arrived at the causeway at about the same time on Good Friday morning. As both the tide and the date of Easter are determined by the moon, the crossing time is the same every year, which gives the pilgrims a frisson of cosmic synchronicity. Before heading off along the Pilgrims' Way, marked by several dozen posts, most remove their boots to make the final part of the pilgrimage with bare feet. It does not take much imagination to feel the sharp, biting cold of the saltwater on feet that are worn and tired with the week's walking.

More recently, I led a pilgrimage of people from South Shields to the same Holy Island. This involved a couple of hours on a coach rather than a week on foot but, sure enough, the coach stopped at the causeway to put down those who wanted to walk.

I was rather surprised at how many people did. One person told me that the last time she had done this was in 1960. Another, who proved herself to be one of the briskest walkers, was well into her eighties. After we got out of the coach, people set off in small groups or on their own, finding their way from post to post. As I took my place in this raggle-taggle procession, it seemed to me that this short pilgrimage, or 'plodge' as it is called locally, is a wonderful metaphor for Christian life. For instance, while would-be pilgrims think that they will be walking across pleasant sand, they soon find that they are walking across slippery mud. One poor man fell over four times. Occasionally there is a little stream to paddle through and sometimes there are gritty areas with lots of broken shells. In other places you have no choice but to walk through thick green seaweed in which the feet and ankles are lost. What the Lindisfarne pilgrim finds on the causeway, so all Christian pilgrims find on the journey of life. We hope to walk across warm, firm and golden sand but often find ourselves in slippery mud or mysterious seaweed. At such times it matters very much that there are people ahead of us, behind us and beside us. We need people who will stand by us when we slip and who will risk slipping to help us when we fall. Another point derives from the fact that this Pilgrim Way is tidal. For this reason it must be one of the very few footpaths in the world which is never marked by the erosive impact of many feet. However many pilgrims walk across, the footprints are washed away every time the tide comes in (together with any dawdling pilgrims, I suppose). There is a lesson in this too. Some people like to think that they are walking a new path. Others prefer the assurance that they are following tradition. Both are true when we walk the pilgrim way through life. The way of Jesus is simultaneously the way of the saints and our own special journey.

The plodge across the causeway to Lindisfarne is not the only example of barefoot pilgrimage, even in the British Isles. Take a walk up Croagh Patrick near Wexford in County Mayo, Ireland's Holy Mountain, and you will see people struggling on the shale with shoes tied around their necks and rosaries in their hands. At Walsingham, people leave their shoes at the Slipper Chapel before the final mile of pilgrimage. Shoes are never worn in mosques or Hindu temples. It is salutary for Christians to enter these places and to have to go through the unusual business of stooping or bending to take off their shoes. The practice is normal in Christian places of worship in some countries and cultures. When assisting a priest at a church in South India, I was a bit puzzled when he said, 'You can leave your chappels by the door'. Until, that is, I saw a collection of flip-flops and sandals and realized that 'chappel' is the generic Tamil word for light footwear. As soon as I could, I shook off my flip-flops and added them to the messy pile. Removing our shoes, and, if we have them, socks, inculcates a different attitude from walking into a sacred space without a pause, or briskly brushing shoes on coconut matting. Many ancient churches still have boot scrapers outside, a testimony to the days when there was considerably less paving and most folk travelled by foot. But it is a very different thing to scrape your boots than to remove them. Following the way of Christ with humility does not involve scraping the mud from our boots. It involves, maybe even requires, that we encounter the earth as barefoot disciples and pilgrims. And so I want to suggest 'Barefoot discipleship' as a metaphor for *passionate humility*, a Christlike attitude that is down-to-earth, full of life, vulnerable and transformative.

Being barefoot is a biblical theme. When Moses was called aside to see and engage with the burning bush, one of his first instructions was, 'Come no closer. Remove your sandals, for the place where you are standing is holy ground' (Exodus 3.5). A less well known barefoot occasion is encountered in the book of Joshua when Joshua has a vision of an angel with a drawn sword. That angel's command is similar: 'Remove the sandals from your feet, for the place where you stand is holy' (Joshua 5.15). The prophet Isaiah walked 'naked and barefoot' for three years (Isaiah 20.3) and, as a result, Isaiah is often shown barefoot in religious art. In Luke chapter 10 Jesus sends the 'seventy others' out in pairs: 'Go on your way. See, I am sending you out like lambs into the midst of wolves. Carry no purse, no bag, no sandals; and greet no one on the road' (Luke 10.4). While most would read this passage as forbidding the taking of an *extra* pair of sandals, some have taken it to mean no sandals at all. Francis and Clare of Assisi are the most obvious examples. To them can be added: Saint Teresa of Ávila, who founded the 'barefoot Carmelites'; Ignatius Loyola, the founder of the Jesuits; Dominic, founder of the Dominicans; Leo Tolstoy, the Russian writer; and George Fox, founder of the Society of Friends.

Walking carefully and barefoot can be a profound form of meditation. This is how Barbara Brown Taylor, a contemporary spiritual writer and priest, describes the walking meditation of a Buddhist monk:

First the bare heel extends over the earth, coming down so slowly that not even a dry leaf is displaced. Then the arch begins its long descent, laying itself down like a cat. Finally the toes arrive, beginning with the small one and ending with the big. Imperceptibly, the arrival turns into a departure as one heel rises and the other comes down.[1]

To watch this, she says, is like watching a 'lunar eclipse', suggesting perhaps that there is deep silence and gentleness in this engagement with gravity and matter. Taylor goes on to commend going barefoot as a spiritual practice:

> Take off your shoes and feel the earth under your feet, as if the ground on which you are standing really is holy ground. Let it please you. Let it hurt you a little. Feel how the world really feels when you do not strap little tanks on your feet to shield you from the way things really are.[2]

Being barefoot requires us to take seriously, and perhaps re-negotiate, our relationship with the earth, the ground on which we walk. Those who are barefoot feel and respond to the earth itself. Being barefoot often means that sensitive skin is exposed and will soon be scratched and bruised. Our attention is drawn to this point of contact, the connection between ourself and the earth. We experience in a new or deeper way both our vulnera-bility and our connectedness.

People who have plenty of shoes to choose from have much to learn by slipping them off for a while and engaging in some attentive walking. But thinking across the human family we soon appreciate that going barefoot is rarely a matter of choice. On the whole, people wear shoes to the extent to which they can afford to wear shoes. In this way shoes have become a symbol of human pride and achievement; the absence of shoes is seen as a sign of poverty and shame. In Frank McCourt's memoir of a childhood growing up in Ireland, *Angela's Ashes*, there is an episode where Angela's husband nails pieces of rubber tyre to the boys' shoes because they have been leaking and he is too proud to see them beg for a replacement pair. His work is clumsy and, on their way to school, the brothers are ribbed and teased, even by poorer boys who are themselves barefoot. Before they arrive at school they take off the shoes but their schoolmaster knows that these are not really barefoot boys and makes them fetch and put on their unwieldy shoes. Then he turns on the class.

> There is sneering here . . . Is there anyone in this class that comes from a rich family with money galore to spend on shoes? . . . There are boys here who have to mend their shoes whatever way they can. . . . There are boys in this class with no shoes at all. It's not their fault and it's no shame. Our Lord had no shoes. He died shoeless. Do you see Him hanging on the cross sporting shoes? Do you, boys?[3]

The class is silenced. The teacher threatens them with the all-too-familiar corporal punishment should anyone be shamed for being poor, and some equilibrium is re-established. It is a telling episode. Suddenly it is not the suffering of the dying Christ that is in focus but his poverty and, by implication, his identification with the poor of the earth. Similarly, the down-to-earth Barefoot Disciple is working out a relationship with God, the poor and the earth while walking in the way of Christ.

Learning to Walk

One of the most charming phases of human development is when a child is learning to walk. Having pushed herself to her feet and learnt how to balance, in a wobbly sort of way, it is not long before she is moving about, holding on to fingers and furniture to steady herself. Then, one day, there is the bold step of adventure when the toddler takes her first toddle, the would-be walker takes his first step. Sometimes the first few paces lead to the security of waiting arms. Equally often, both on the first solo steps and in the many little journeys that follow, the little one falls unceremoniously to the ground. There might be tears at this point, but infant tears do not carry the emotional gravitas of adult ones. They are a shout for help and are soon dried as knees and elbows are rubbed and kissed better. Thus the child learns, by trial and error, to walk. Essentially, they teach themselves. Parents enjoy being witness to the great event rather than feel themselves to be teachers. They worry about being there when it happens, not about being there to make it happen.

When adults have to learn how to walk it is a very different story. They start from a different place. Normally, they will be trying to recover a skill and ability that has been lost. That is bad enough. What is worse is that they are so tall. Not only is their centre of gravity much higher, making balance more difficult to achieve, but there is so much further to fall. It is a much riskier business. It does not help that the skill of walking is such an automatic skill that we rarely reflect on it and so do not realize how complex it is. Generally speaking, adult walkers do not think much at all about what they are doing. They just do it. This is wonderful until there is a need to learn how to walk again; until there is a need to walk consciously. For instance, one thing that I did not realize until a physiotherapist pointed it out to me, is that walking happens because we briefly put ourselves off-balance and start to topple forward until we break our fall with our front foot. If you do not believe this then stand up and try to walk deliberately. Start with two feet on the ground. Then raise one. As you move that foot forward you have to throw yourself slightly off-balance before it hits the ground a stride ahead. As you do this self-consciously, you will soon notice how uncomfortable and ungainly it is. Most of the time we only dare to put ourselves off-balance and fall forward because we do not realize that this is what we are doing.

Much adult learning reflects this dynamic. Ask anyone who has learnt to ride a bicycle or to swim or who has attempted a musical instrument in adulthood and they will tell you a story of risk and humiliation. They probably will not use that language, but that is what they will be speaking about. Humility is the virtue that allows people to take the risks and survive the humiliation. And just as it underpins the learning of practical skills, so it is integral to the task of learning discipleship. What seems easy for a child is risky and scary for a grown-up. What can feel very straightforward when you do not think about it, can feel very difficult when you put it through your conscious mind. That is one reason why, as we strive to become more articulate, deliberate and intentional about discipleship, we also need to find ways to articulate that faith in jargon-free language and to live it out in unself-conscious service and through the practice of deep, semi-automatic habits. The virtue of humility connects with just this imperative because it is also necessarily unself-conscious. If we ever need to learn how to walk again without thinking, we will have to think very hard about what we are doing until we regain the skill. Learning to walk again is a deliberate and painful effort, however fluent a walker we one day become. Similarly, if we are one day to live with unaffected humility, we might need some of that deliberate, awkward effort, and maybe the help of the spiritual equivalent of a physiotherapist. The snag is that we need a certain amount of humility and wisdom to seek that kind of help, and risk that kind of deliberateness, in the first place.

Washing Feet

The most striking example of humility in the Gospels is the occasion when Jesus washed his disciples' feet. As the evangelist John makes clear, this was both a practical act of service and an example to be followed:

Now before the festival of the Passover, Jesus knew that his hour had come to depart from this world and go to the Father. Having loved his own who were in the world, he loved them to the end. The devil had already put it into the heart of Judas son of Simon Iscariot to betray him. And during supper Jesus, knowing that the Father had given all things into his hands, and that he had come from God and was going to God, got up from the table, took off his outer robe, and tied a towel around himself. Then he poured water into a basin and began to wash the disciples' feet and to wipe them with the towel that was tied around him. (John 13.1–5)

The foot-washing constitutes an invitation not only to learn a lesson but also to follow an example. It is recorded and re-enacted not only to provoke our admiration but our emulation. It is meant to touch our imaginations and to set us wondering: 'Could I do that?', 'Would I do that?', 'Should I do that?', and '*Shall* I do that?' Jesus' example is meant to challenge our aspirations; to suggest to us that we could learn how to do this. Ann Morisy suggests that such questions are integral to community ministry which purposefully works for the kingdom of God. This involves not seeking to meet the needs to the poor on our own terms but *envisioning* a radically different future.[4] They are the sort of questions that embolden people to face reality and enter into the vulnerability of risk-taking. This is the point of the foot-washing. It is not that the feet needed a wash, but that the disciples needed a new set of attitudes. Discipleship might seem to involve meeting the needs of others but at a more radical level it is about doing the things that cause us to be changed in heart and mind. Focusing on the needs of others is a tried and tested way out of excessive self-concern and interest. But it only works, so to speak, if it leads us to discover that the other has more to offer us than we them. This is the flip-side of the famous quote that if you want to change the world you must start with yourself. The reality is that if you seriously go about trying to change the world for the better, you yourself will be more profoundly transformed in the process than 'the world'. I wonder whether it is too much to call that transformation 'being humbled'. Certainly those who engage with passion and empathy in the cause of justice often speak of being humbled when they come up for air. We should cheer when they do so, and seek the path of our own humbling.

While on sabbatical in South Africa in 2002, I attended the Maundy Thursday service for the clergy of the diocese of Cape Town. I was treated as an honoured guest. 'You will wear a cope, Father. And sit at the front, Father. It is good that you are with us, Father.' After the service I was sent to have a lunch of hot-dogs and soup with the bishops. It was an honour, but my friends were all parish clergy and they were eating together in a large hall not far away. I realized that day that the higher place was not necessarily a more congenial or comfortable place. After the lunch I drove out to the coastal village which I will call Sandton where I was to learn that the lowest place is not entirely straightforward or without issues either.

Under apartheid, Sandton was a 'coloured' area and the village reflects this history not only in its demography, but also in the legacy of drug-related crime and violence. When I had been there before to meet the priest, I will call him Andrew, the vicarage had just been burgled. This was a real shock because, together with several other incidents, it suggested that the traditional taboo protecting the clergy was dying, if not dead. As drugs became more and more a part of the culture of the village, so law and order and tradition were all breaking down. This meant that there was a high level of fear and anxiety. For instance, the (white) organist from the neighbouring town was no longer prepared to take the risk of coming into the village to play for services, so the weekend that I was there, the services were unaccompanied.

As Andrew and I talked through the service for the evening it became clear that he saw me taking a very significant role. I had prepared a sermon but had not anticipated what he offered next. 'I think it would be good, if you were happy with it, for you to do the foot-washing.' It was an odd moment. I was delighted but apprehensive. Several years later, a person told me that she was beginning to feel that she was being called to ordained ministry. 'I like the idea, but it just scares me', she said. I think that is exactly what I felt. Trepidation is the word. Trepidation about getting down on the floor of the church in the middle of a Communion service on Maundy Thursday and self-consciously imitating and performing the action of Jesus as recorded in John's Gospel. And yet within a few hours I took the towel and the water and, shuffling along on the floor, washed the feet of twelve people whom I had never met before. It was an experience of ritualized intimacy and real privilege. The feet were sandy and dirty and gave plenty of evidence of having had a hard life. All were calloused. Some were misshapen. All were simply slipped out of their sandals. Having washed and dried each foot, I did as the priest had indicated was the custom, and kissed it before I shuffled on to the next person. It was a charged and sacred moment, but as I moved about on the floor the name of a person whose funeral I conducted as a curate well over a decade previously came to mind. It was a Mr Shufflebottom ('Now there's a great Lancashire name,' said the funeral director).

Today, the ministry pages of the Church of England's website carry a photograph of the Archbishop of Canterbury washing feet at a Maundy Thursday Eucharist. When he did this in 2003, he was the first Archbishop of Canterbury to do so since the Reformation. A cathedral official saw this as a great photo opportunity and the image was on the front pages on Good Friday. Up until the eighteenth century the monarch had also done this, as well as giving a few specially minted coins known as Maundy money. The money ceremony continues to this day. It is popular and, it must be said, less problematic than foot-washing, partly because it does not seem to be an attempt to perform humility. The ritual always carries the danger of being a pious apeing of the real thing. While this would always be a travesty, it would have been an especially painful one in Sandton where I was a white visitor in a church full of people who, for most of their lives, had been taught that they were so different from white people that they could neither live nor worship with them.

In Sandton, the twelve sat on chairs to have their feet washed. This set them above me in a very literal way. This is different from the way a podiatrist or chiropodist works and is more like the diminutive position of one who cleans shoes on the street. Notice how high the seats are of those who avail themselves of such service. I am sure that this is in part for the benefit of the workers: to save them having to bend quite so low or sit on the floor. But it has the effect of making those who sit seem very grand. An impression forced onto me on one of the occasions when I saw this taking place reinforced this point. The person in question was a young man who was smoking a very large cigar. You could feel the air of superiority five metres away. It was neither an edifying nor an encouraging sight. It did nothing to warm the heart. To witness humility, on the other hand, does all three. That is why we delight to see it in others even if we find it hard to imagine it in ourselves, or for that matter even to aspire to it. However, as I have stressed, humility is not an optional extra for especially good or virtuous people, but is the essence not only of Christian ministry, but also of Christian discipleship.

The story of Jesus washing his disciples' feet is in John 13. But John 12 offers an interesting parallel which I want to suggest that we read as a preparation for it. Jesus was a guest at the house of Mary, Martha and Lazarus when a meal was held in his honour. While Martha served and Lazarus shared in the meal, Mary did something profoundly memorable. 'Mary took a pound of costly perfume made of pure nard, anointed Jesus' feet, and wiped them with her hair' (John 12.3). Is it reasonable to suggest that Jesus' humility was evident as much in Chapter 12 as in Chapter 13? That there was just as much humility involved in being anointed as in washing others? The anointing was a reference to his forthcoming death. That's another connection with humility. It is genuinely humble to recognize that we are mortal and that sooner or later death will be upon us. For humility involves accepting just this level of gritty, down-to-earth, bodily reality. Humility is the virtue of seeing, saying and feeling things in a straightforward way, a way full of the grace and truth that John's Gospel sees in Jesus, the Word made flesh. Grace and truth embrace in the incarnation – in Jesus Christ the God-human. And they meet in what we might call ordinary humility. That may sound like a grand claim. But it is, in truth, a modest and appropriate one. Grace and truth certainly do not connect in arrogance. For even when it is right, arrogance is ugly and graceless.

Jesus was teaching the disciples a lesson when he washed their feet. Moreover, he was teaching not with words but by example. It was less a didactic and more a transformational moment. It marked a transition in his relationship with his followers and, as a result or consequence of this, there needed to be a new relationship *between* those followers. Inevitably this had to be put into words. But as the action and memory of the foot-washing remind us, it is the action which is always primary. Brian Wren's hymn, 'Lord God, your love has called us here' makes the point:

Then take the towel and break the bread
And humble us and call us friends.[5]

The temptation to romanticize this is very strong. Herbert Kelly, founder of the Society of the Sacred Mission, was alert to this when he wrote in his *Principles*, 'Many read of washing the disciples' feet, who think themselves above cleaning another man's boots.'[6] Ministry is nothing as long as it is a theory, and yet, when it becomes a humble practice, it can be a powerful force for good, an announcement and an anticipation of God's kingdom. Jesus had to be proactive and imaginative in order to wash the feet of his disciples, but what he initiated was his own contact with dirty, tired, sensitive, symbolic feet. When we find the humility to follow in this way, we cross a series of boundaries and enter into a new moral and spiritual universe, the place where Christ reigns. But even as we do so we need to be alert to some of the 'mind games', or even 'soul games', that tend to get played out inside us.

When Jesus' washing of his disciples' feet is re-enacted in liturgy, it is public performance by a person in role. This means that it is not an act of humility on the part of the person who is playing that role. Rather, it is a statement about the spiritual power of the action being recalled and the value being placed on such humility. Clergy and lay people need always to remember that liturgical foot-washing is not about the virtue or otherwise of the minister involved. Should anyone suggest that it is, then others are right to be suspicious. 'Playing Jesus' in a service might seem to be a small price to pay for 'playing God' for the rest of the time! But there is another point too. As someone once said to me, 'There is no shortage of priests who are happy to emulate Jesus in a service by washing people's feet. It's finding the people who are happy to have their feet washed which is more difficult.' There are several layers of truth in this, one of which concerns the centrality of humility in Christian discipleship. For it is the disciples who had their feet washed. Peter, typically, could not get his head around this. But there was nothing complex to understand. Having your feet washed is all about receiving. What makes it difficult is that we cannot receive this gift without adjusting in a profound and deep way. To have one's feet washed is a formative experience.

Notes

1. Taylor, *An Altar in the World*, p. 60.
2. Taylor, *An Altar in the World*, p. 67.
3. McCourt, *Angela's Ashes*, p. 116.
4. Morisy, *Beyond the Good Samaritan*, p. 33.
5. *Hymns Ancient and Modern (New Standard)*, no. 489.
6. Unpublished pamphlet.

CHAPTER 3

A Terrible Force

In the twelfth century, Bernard of Clairvaux was asked by Godfrey of Langres to write about humility. He found it a far from straightforward assignment and, in the end, wrote more about pride. His reasoning was that, as a sinner, he felt that he knew more about pride than humility. His pen-portraits of monks who get caught up in proud ways can still speak to us today. He is acute in his observations of talkative monks who love to boast of their religious fervour. 'He warmly recommends fasting, urges watching and exalts prayer above all. He will give a long discourse on patience and humility and each of the other virtues – all words, all bragging.'[1] It is worrying stuff. There are so many ways to get it wrong that it might, after all, be better to take a vow of silence on the subject of humility. But Bernard's warnings are not against reaching out to others with generosity of spirit. They are about being a prat.

Michael Ramsey is perhaps a little more sympathetic when addressing men about to be ordained. He outlines just how easy it is *not* to grow in humility:

There will be everything in the world to thwart you. If you do well, you can be pleased with yourself, and humility is in peril. If you do badly, you may worry about yourself, and humility is in peril. If people are nice to you and tell you what a good clergyman you are, humility is in peril. If people are nasty to you, you have a grievance, and humility is in peril. Furthermore, the temptations to jealousy between us in the ministry are more subtle and common than you may realize. So too, if you are learning to be humble you are in peril. You can half-consciously congratulate your self that you are a spiritually minded priest unlike the worldly, pompous, ill-trained Erastian clergyman in the next parish. We all know some of the caricatures of a man who, knowing he is meant to be humble, affects it in mannerisms of speech and habit.[2]

Ramsey is clear-eyed about the perils, the possibility of self-delusion (the half-conscious self-congratulation) and the truth that mannered humility is not humility at all. But none of this means that humility is an inappropriate spiritual and ethical quest. It just underlines how difficult and demanding it is.

Humility is a biblical and traditional Christian virtue. It features prominently in our understanding of both the actions and the teachings of Jesus. In the most important New Testament passage on this subject, Paul encourages the Christians of Philippi to adopt the same 'mind' that was in Christ Jesus (Philippians 2.5). Some scholars helpfully suggest that the word 'mind' here might more helpfully be translated 'attitude'. 'Like Christ Jesus, have a humble attitude' is a good way of putting it. Paul goes on to quote words which are thought to be from a very early hymn and so rank as some of the earliest, if not *the* earliest words in the New Testament.

[Christ Jesus] who, though he was in the form of God,
   did not regard equality with God as something to be exploited,
but emptied himself,
   taking the form of a slave,

being born in human likeness.
And being found in human form, he humbled himself
and became obedient to the point of death –
even death on a cross.

Therefore God also highly exalted him
and gave him the name
that is above every name,
so that at the name of Jesus
every knee should bend,
in heaven and earth and under the earth,
and every tongue should confess
that Jesus Christ is Lord
to the glory of God the Father. (Philippians 2.6–11)

This hymn does not in itself give a working definition of humility
that can guide the details of our living. Rather, it serves the same
multiple purposes as all hymns, which are to articulate praise,
build up fellowship and at the same time challenge and inspire
each individual who gives them voice. This hymn offers inspi-
ration to develop and *inhabit* a humble attitude. Such an attitude
is also characterized by the short lists of personal qualities found
in several of the New Testament epistles. In the letter to the
Colossian Christians, for instance, having first invited them to
divest themselves of five inappropriate behaviours, Paul lists five
which are far more becoming. 'As God's chosen ones, holy and
beloved, clothe yourselves with compassion, kindness, humility,
meekness and patience' (Colossians 3.12). Peter offers a similar
package when he writes, 'Finally, all of you, have unity of Spirit,
sympathy, love for one another, a tender heart and a humble
mind' (1 Peter 3.8). The same pattern is seen in Ephesians, 'I . . .
beg you to lead a life worthy of the calling to which you have been

called, with all humility and gentleness, with patience, bearing with one another in love, making every effort to maintain the unity of the spirit in the bond of peace' (Ephesians 4.1–3).

These lists point to a personality or character that is *inspired* by the testimony and teaching of the Gospel and which *aspires* to the cluster of behaviours, attitudes, values and practices that are summarized in the word 'Christlike'. This word has come to refer to the way in which Jesus revealed the humility of God. Michael Ramsey, for instance, famously wrote that 'God is Christ-like, and in him is no un-Christlikeness at all.'[3] Although he knew how problematic and difficult it is, Ramsey also insisted that personal humility is integral to priestly ministry. Writing decades before women were first ordained, he put it like this:

> . . . there is only one kind of *person* who makes God known and realized by other people, and that is the person who is humble because he knows God and knows God because he is humble. There is no substitute for this. It is only a humble priest who is authoritatively a man of God, one who makes God real to his fellows. May it one day be said of you, not necessarily that you talked about God cleverly, but that you made God real to people. 'He somehow made God real to me': only humility can do that.[4]

The Rule of St Benedict is perhaps the greatest sustained attempt to encourage and enable people to grow in humility. Benedict's approach is anchored in Jesus' teaching that: '. . . all who exalt themselves will be humbled, and those who humble themselves will be exalted' (Luke 14.11). The Benedictine monk and writer, Michael Casey, emphasizes that this is not about seeking reward but letting holy desire shape character and attitude.

Humility is that network of attitudes that springs from a radical conversion of heart, and signals a deep, inner conformity with Christ. Growth in humility is powered by the simple desire to become like Christ.[5]

The humility which the Rule of St Benedict seeks to inculcate is a profoundly down-to-earth attitude. His ascent to humility is not a disembodied spiritual practice but something holistic: a matter of both soul and body. Some commentators suggest that it is better to think of Benedict's key instructions on the subject as being about an exploration not of humility so much as into *reality*: 'into the reality of being earthed in myself and in God'.[6] The derivation of the word 'humility' is the same as 'humus', which is the product of the long, slow and apparently negative but vital process of decomposition or decay. Like humus, humility is produced by ordinary, often unnoticed, protracted and deeply unromantic processes. Genuine attempts to describe humility, and honest efforts to live humbly, point us away from fantasy and towards reality. They bring us down to earth. Humility is the *earthiest* of the virtues. It is not about being pious; it is about being grounded. It is not concerned with being esoteric but ordinary. It is also honest and, in subtle ways, self-aware.

Selfless Respect for Reality

André Comte-Sponville sees honesty as the key to humility and suggests it involves being alert to our limits. 'Being humble means loving the truth and submitting to it. Humility means loving truth more than oneself.'[7] Robert Roberts also puts a high premium on honesty as a component of humility which he sees as entirely consistent with self-confidence, initiative and assertiveness. It is honesty about who we are, robust self-awareness, that he sees in the genuinely humble person. He expresses this carefully:

> Humility is the ability, without prejudice to one's self-comfort to admit one's inferiority, in this or that respect to another. And it is the ability, without increment to one's self-comfort or prejudice to the quality of one's relationship with another, to remark one's superiority, in this or that respect to another . . . [it is] an emotional independence of one's judgements concerning how one ranks vis-à-vis other human beings.[8]

Humility in this sense allows us to rank ourselves positively or negatively with regard to others but without rancour. Such humility puts an end to what we might call the 'meekness competition', in which everyone vies for the lowest place because they see it as the most advantageous position from which to compete for the highest place. Roberts' deeper concern, however, is precisely to get beyond any sense of competition for self-worth. This he calls 'spiritual cannibalism', the habit of generating our own sense of moral dignity at the expense of the repute of others. Understood properly, humility will take us well beyond such an attitude and its all too common practices.

In her essay *The Sovereignty of Good*, Iris Murdoch suggests that humility is the virtue which 'clears our mind of selfish care'.[9] It is the virtue which helps us overcome the self-regarding and anxious habits of mind which shield us from reality. Humility, aided by sympathetic imagination, frees us from self-obsessed anxiety and enables us to turn our attention outwards so that we become more other-aware than self-aware. Humility is not a negative way of regarding the self but a positive way of regarding reality. It involves forgetting ourselves and directing our attention outwards. I believe that this is a very helpful way of looking at it but that it is more difficult than it at first seems. For most of us this is a profound spiritual struggle. We find the path to other-awareness and self-forgetfulness to be a long and difficult one and, unless we are very exceptional, we will never arrive at the goal. Attending to God increases our desire to attend to other people but, again and again, much to our annoyance and spiritual frustration, we become the subject of our own thoughts. There is no getting away from this, no short-circuiting of our self-regard. And that is why it is wise to aspire to humility not as a form of self-improvement, but as a virtue that befits those who seek the kingdom of God. However, the growing pains of discipleship can be quite excruciating.

We need to be very realistic about this. The ideal of self-forgetfulness will never be ours and so we need to come to terms with our self-regard. The truth, I suspect, is that while humility does take us beyond self-concern, self-awareness is part of the process of learning humility. To seek to be humble is to seek to become the kind of person who develops what we might call proportional or healthy self-awareness. That is, enough self-awareness to allow us to begin to forget ourselves and give our attention to others.

Let me put this in terms of an analogy. When we are over-tired we find it difficult to fall asleep. Our minds go round and round in circles and we get more and more anxious and self-obsessed. This is frustrating and distressing and yet we are powerless to do anything about it unless we can summon up enough energy to allow the brain to clear itself, rather like the way a windscreen-wiper clears rain from a windscreen. So it is with self-awareness and humility. Looking through the windscreen of life, our vision is obscured by the raindrops of self-awareness. We become more and more the subject of our own attention until, whoosh, the wiper-blade of humility sweeps them to one side. The insomniac who summons up the energy to read a book that draws the attention away from the ever-circling and over-anxious thoughts of the small hours does something similar. However, there are no automatic windscreen-wipers on our soul and we can no more make ourselves humble than we can make ourselves go to sleep. It can only happen if we *stop* trying to achieve it. And yet, that does not mean that we do not wash our teeth and climb between the sheets.

We cannot make ourselves humble, but that does not mean that we should not aspire to humility. Robert Roberts commends humility precisely as a 'moral project' which involves attempting to cultivate an 'evenhanded, deep self-confidence'.[10] The kind which is grounded in honesty and which is based neither on comparison with others nor, most importantly, our feelings.

> Humility itself is not an emotion, like joy or gratitude or contrition. A person could be a wonderful exemplar of humility without ever feeling humble; in fact, one who frequently feels humble is probably not very humble. But humility is an emotion-disposition – primarily a negative one, a disposition *not* to feel the emotions associated with caring a lot about one's status. As an inclination to construe as my equal every person who is presented to me, humility is a disposition not to be downcast by the fact that someone is clearly ahead of me in the games of the world nor to find any satisfaction in noting that I am ahead of someone in those games . . . It is thus a self-confidence, one that runs far deeper than the tenuous self-confidence of the person who believes in himself because others look up to him.[11]

We must be careful here because we can misread Roberts to suggest that humility is a kind of aloofness or effortless superiority. It is not that. But nor is it effortful inferiority. It is a gentler, calmer, more modest business than either. It is honest and informed self-awareness, and as such it is always partial and incomplete, a work in progress. For growth in humility is not a project in self-improvement; it is an attempt to open ourselves more fully both to God's will and to reality. To put it more theologically, true humility is acutely and profoundly aware of the promise, the presence and the absence of the kingdom of God and the tension between them. And it is this awareness which makes it both self-forgetful and deeply passionate.

Saint Benedict knew that humility was the key virtue for monks. But humility is not something which is only relevant in the peaceful and contemplative order of the cloister. It is a robust attitude that carries a difference-making, transformative edge in everyday life. I want to suggest that humility is most Christlike when it combines a certain down-to-earth acceptance of reality with a passionate longing for God's kingdom of justice, truth, mercy and peace. As Dostoyevsky's sage, Father Zossima, saw, such true humility has transformative power.

> At some ideas you stand perplexed, especially the sight of other men's sins, asking yourself whether to combat them by force or by humble love. Always decide, 'I will combat it by humble love.' If you make up your mind about that once and for all, you will be able to conquer the whole world. Loving humility is a terrible force, the strongest of all, there is nothing like it.[12]

A humble attitude is not a weak or ineffective one. Rather, it is confident enough to seek truth and justice with sincere and selfless hope and determination. It is a 'terrible force'. What it is not is grand, arrogant or overly self-regarding. If this is right, and humility does have power, it must be of interest to those who carry responsibility and exercise leadership. But what is the connection?

Leadership and Humility

Robert Greanleaf coined the phrase 'servant leadership' to describe the attitude of a leader who honours and respects those who are being led, and who puts him- or herself into the task of caring for those who, while more lowly in the organization, are perhaps closer to the front line. The phrase might be his but the concept is not new. Neither is it explicitly Christian, although Jesus washing his disciples' feet is often offered as a great example of servant leadership in practice. Humility and leadership are connected in ancient Chinese Taoist teachings which emphasize that great leadership is more content with silence and gentle guidance than with forcing something through by dint of strong personality or positional power.[13] Jim Collins picked up on the importance of humility in his study of what makes the difference between the good and the great in the corporate world.[14] He has identified it as an intrinsic quality of what he calls 'Level 5 Leadership'. To grasp what Collins is talking about we need briefly to survey the other four levels. His scheme begins with a 'highly capable individual' and then moves to 'contributing team player'. At level 3 we find the 'competent manager'. Level 4 brings us to the 'effective leader' who can elevate the performance of others by galvanizing them with a clear and compelling vision. What, then, is there to add at the higher level? His first point is that those at level 5 will still need to function at the four lower levels. The needs which those skills and abilities meet do not go away. The difference is that level 5 leaders 'channel their ego needs away from themselves and into the larger goal of building a great company'.[15] Interestingly, Collins' research team stumbled across this finding despite the fact that he had all but ruled out 'leadership' as a component in corporate greatness. Indeed, he told his researchers to 'ignore the executives', presumably believing that many are strong personalities who got where they are today not by making a difference to outcomes so much as by persuading others of their singular contribution to previous successful ventures. However, it became clear in their research that leadership *is* a major factor, but not in a clichéd or predictable way. Truly great leaders are characterized not by overt 'strength of personality' or 'presence' but by 'humility'. 'Level 5 leaders display a compelling modesty, are self-effacing and understated'.[16]

Collins believes that level 5 leadership qualities are not rare in society but that they are not found as often as they might be in business leaders. The reason seems to be that level 4 leaders are better at competing for the top jobs because they approximate more closely to our naïve understanding of what 'strong leadership' looks like. All too often we look for self-belief when we would be wiser to seek out genuine humility. This has serious consequences, as Collins observes: 'One of the most damaging trends in recent history is the tendency (especially by boards of directors) to select dazzling, celebrity leaders and to de-select potential Level 5 leaders.'[17]

David Owen, the former Labour Foreign Secretary, co-founder of the Social Democratic Party and medical doctor, has examined the way in which power can go to the heads of political leaders. Looking at this in the context of studying the health and disease of those who have held high political office, he suggests that some develop what he calls 'hubristic syndrome'. He lists a number of symptoms and suggests that those with hubristic syndrome manifest three or four of them. The list identifies various behaviours, attitudes and beliefs, many of which are attitudes of self-regard: narcissism, messianic sense of self, use of the royal 'we', disproportionate concern with image and presentation, unshakeable belief that they will be vindicated.[18] It boils down to extraordinary and unassailable self-confidence which leads to a lack of listening and attention to any details which might dent their all-powerful narcissism. While he calls this 'hubristic syndrome' we might also call it the 'eclipse of humility syndrome'. For humility is what is missing. This matters very much. For without humility, leadership is a very dodgy and dangerous business. If we are interested in forming leaders, we should put at least as much effort into helping them learn humility as anything else. For it is the virtue of humility which has the capacity to transform a narcissistic enjoyment of power and position which is often apparent only to those who are *not* in a position to do anything about it.

Humility, then, is an important and powerful virtue. However, as we have seen, the word 'humility' comes with excess baggage and so distorts the Christlike image and bends our values unhelpfully. Indeed for Collins, humility is not the only ingredient of level 5 leadership. It is part of it, but it is not the whole story. 'Level 5 Leaders are modest *and wilful*, humble *and fearless*.'[19] Humility alone is not enough, which is why Collins does not talk of 'selfless leaders' or 'servant leaders'. Level 5 leaders are passionately engaged. In the business world they are highly motivated on behalf of their company. They know that to lead a successful venture they must be wise in discerning when to step forward and when to step back, when to speak and when to listen. Great leaders are humble enough to realize that if it 'all depends on me' then the project itself, and indeed the achievement at the end of the day, will be modest, even if they end up looking and feeling big.

All this supports the suggestion that if we are to talk about humility as a Christian virtue today, we will be well advised to qualify it. Collins has much to say that might help us develop Christian leadership. We could, for instance, speak of 'Level 5 Ministry', which would be modest but determined, down-to-earth yet passionate for the kingdom of God. Such ministry would not be anxious about status but would be hungry for the fruit of the Spirit and thirsty for justice. Dostoyevsky's Father Zossima spoke of 'loving humility'. That's not the same as the motivation to see the company succeed that Collins is talking about, but we can see it on the same spectrum. Maybe *passionate humility* comes somewhere between Zossima's 'loving humility' and Collins' combination of humility and 'fearlessness'. Passionate humility is humility with attitude, humility with edge. Passionate humility implies radical openness and costly vulnerability. Passionate humility knows something about the kingdom of God, and desires it deeply.

Making an Entry

One year, I led a Palm Sunday procession from a Victorian church destined to close, to an ancient parish church whose life would be transformed by the influx of the small, elderly, but committed and friendly congregation that had worshipped at the closing church. I recall how moving it was when we stopped outside the flat of a frail member of one of the congregations and prayed not only for her but for all the people living in those flats. Another year I was in Cape Town. My memories of that are dominated by the baking heat and the beautiful view of Table Mountain as the guitar-playing priest led the congregation around the desolate area called District Six: a once thriving multi-ethnic community that was razed to the ground in the apartheid years. Later that day I attended what was billed as a 'passion play' at a church on the Cape Flats. It was a compilation of songs from

Godspell and *Jesus Christ Superstar* performed by the church choir. The choirmaster and organist, a very large man, cast himself as Jesus. When it came to the Palm Sunday scene, this Jesus was propelled on to the stage in a supermarket trolley. No one could keep a straight face. It said something amusing but true about Jesus and the ordinary things of everyday life. Another year I was in Rome. As we approached St Peter's Square the crowds became thicker, and on every street corner young people were selling olive branches and green palm crosses to raise money for charity. The Mass itself began with an awe-inspiring procession around the Square with Pope John Paul at the rear in his 'Pope-mobile' waving at the crowd and palpably drawing energy from them as they waved back; energy that he would return as he devoutly led the service with slurred speech and slumping body. The late Pope remains a controversial figure, as paradoxical as he was holy and as troubling as he was admirable. But whatever else you might say of him, he certainly knew how to make an entry. Like Jesus, he had no fear of the dramatic gesture.

Jesus stage-managed his entry into Jerusalem on the first Palm Sunday. He used it as the occasion to present himself and his mission. It is traditional to call his entry into Jerusalem the 'triumphal entry' and the phrase is often used as a subheading for the relevant Bible passages (Matthew 21.1–11, Mark 11.1–11, Luke 19.28–40). This is because of the allusion to the prophet Zechariah in Matthew's version. However, when Matthew quoted the prophet Zechariah he did so selectively. This is the relevant verse: 'Lo, your king comes to you; triumphant and victorious is he, humble and riding on a donkey, on a colt, the foal of a donkey' (Zechariah 9.9). When he wrote about Palm Sunday, Matthew left out the words 'triumph' and 'victory' and cut straight to the word 'humble' (Matthew 21.5). This observation leads me to wonder why today we invariably refer to Jesus' entry into Jerusalem as 'triumphal'. Might 'humble' not be the more biblical or, at least, the more New Testament, way of looking at it? I want to suggest that we find it hard to think of Jesus' entry into Jerusalem as a humble act because it contradicts our caricatures of humility as fawning, feeble and self-deprecating. The Church looks at Jesus on a donkey and hears the echo of the first half of the verse from Zechariah about triumph and victory but fails to notice that the word *humble* is seen not only as relevant but also appropriate and fitting. Like the shouting crowd, we fail to notice that our values and assumptions are being challenged by this entry. The people are praising the son of David and crying for help: 'Save us! Be our hero.' Despite what they have already heard of Jesus' ministry to date, they are still thinking of victory and triumph; they are still looking for the kind of Messianic leader and liberator whom Jesus is not. They have not yet grasped, as we have not yet grasped, the shape and the form of true Christlikeness that is found in Jesus. They have not yet seen the Christlikeness of passionate humility.

The stage-managing of the entry also contributes to our difficulty in thinking of 'humble' as an apt word to describe it. When we are deliberately presenting ourselves, our humility is rarely our most evident quality. And yet it might be that a Christlike approach to humility not only allows but insists on an honest and committed, a *passionate*, acknowledgement of who we are in our actions and attitudes.

An illustration might draw out some of the tension in this. In the seventeenth century the great painter Peter Paul Rubens presented a painting to Henry Danvers, Earl of Derby. Danvers did not know very much about art and so was unaware that it was a piece only nominally by Rubens himself and mostly done by studio hands. Unbeknown to Rubens, however, the piece was intended as a gift for the then Prince of Wales, who was something of a connoisseur. The Prince took one look at the work and sent it back with the complaint that it was 'not the hand of the master'. Rubens' response to this was to send the Prince an authentic self-portrait.

On hearing this story there are some who feel that this was a proud, pompous or arrogant response. But there is another side to it. The problem with the original painting was that there was nothing of Rubens himself in it. Rubens knew that the prince knew this and wanted to make amends. He decided to give him the works: an image by his own hand of his own face which, as one commentator puts it, 'is staring straight out and saying, I know that you understand great art and know that I am a great artist and here sir, I present myself to you'. There is audacity in that, but do we have to say that it lacked humility because it was so daring? I think not. But this is non-grovelling humility which is robust and confident and yet respectful of others. It is the sort of humility to which we might aspire because we glimpsed it when Jesus of Nazareth made an entry into Jerusalem. It is *passionate humility.*

What happened *after* Jesus' humble entry gives us all the more reason to question the picture of humility that is often painted. The first thing he did was to go into the Temple and let fly. My Bible has the subheading, 'Jesus cleanses the Temple'. 'Jesus makes *a mess of* the Temple' would be nearer the mark. Turning over the tables and shouting is not the sort of behaviour we expect of the humble. We do not expect humble people to get angry. We idly assume that people are beginning to get above themselves or arrogant when they act out of passion. It is not so simple. Maybe the point of Palm Sunday is to help us understand that humility and self-presentation, not to mention humility and passion, can indeed be deeply and profoundly connected. When we begin to think of Jesus' entry into Jerusalem as a genuinely, passionately, *humble* entry, this powerful Christian concept and attitude begins to make sense to us in a deeper way. Palm Sunday points us away from Uriah Heap's cloying, manipulative self-description as ''umble' and towards the passionate humility of true Christian discipleship and prophecy. This sort of humility is assertive and bold. It is energizing and empowering. It is all of a piece with the courage and vulnerability that is revealed on the donkey, in the Temple and ultimately on the cross. Its concern is not to be modest but to be honest, not to be diffident but to be fully present, not to present the self but to put the self on the line for the kingdom of God.

The word 'passion' speaks of energy and determination, excitement and willingness to suffer. It is a hot and sometimes dangerous word. Our passion can be engaged in many ways, good and bad. Passion can spill into greed and lust and reinforce egotistical pride. It can motivate us to be successful, powerful or healthy – or all three. But passionate *humility* is motivated by peace and seeks reconciliation by aspiring to justice while remaining merciful. Passionate humility rages when it sees innocent suffering or falsehood perpetrated, but melts when it encounters true repentance. It is not afraid of anger or conflict or of suffering the consequences of being radically open and undefended. Indeed, the attitude of passionate humility is at a polar extreme to the attitude of personal defensiveness. Why? Because passionate humility is the attitude of those who embrace God's mission and seek God's kingdom. Passionate humility is the virtue of those who know of the promise, the presence and the absence of the kingdom of God. Passionate humility is an attitude which allows us to present and offer ourselves, profoundly limited as we are, in the cause of God's mission.

Notes

1. Bernard of Clairvaux, *The Steps of Humility and Pride*, p. 69.
2. Ramsey, *The Christian Priest Today*, p. 78/9.
3. Ramsey, *God, Christ and the World*, p. 98.
4. Ramsey, *The Christian Priest Today*, p. 78.
5. Casey, *Truthful Living*, p. 10.
6. de Waal, *A Life-Giving Way*, p. 51.
7. Comte-Sponville, *A Small Treatise on the Great Virtues*, p. 141.
8. Roberts, *Spiritual Emotions*, p. 83.
9. Murdoch, *The Sovereignty of Good*, p. 85.
10. Roberts, *Spiritual Emotions*, p. 89.
11. Roberts, *Spiritual Emotions*, p. 88.
12. Dostoyevsky, *The Brothers Karamazov*, p. 376.
13. Adair, *Inspiring Leadership*, pp. 39–44.
14. Collins, *Good to Great*.
15. Collins, *Good to Great*, p. 21.
16. Collins, *Good to Great*, p. 39.
17. Collins, *Good to Great*, p. 39.
18. Owen, *The Hubris Syndrome*, pp. 1–3.
19. Collins, *Good to Great*, p. 22, emphasis mine.

CHAPTER 4

Humiliation, Pride and Modesty

Humiliation

One year, Bill Bryson, Chancellor of Durham University, used his speech at the graduation ceremony in the cathedral to encourage the students to think of how special, blessed and unique they were as individuals. They liked this very much. So did the proud parents. Then he reminded them that the same applies to everyone else on the planet. It is a sound point, intentionally designed gently to bring them down to earth on their big day. It was, if you like, a lesson in humility. It is always a risky business to try to give such a lesson but he got away with it because the overall context of the occasion was a celebration and because it was kindly meant and charmingly put. But such lessons tread the dangerous and meandering boundary between the territories of humility and humiliation. It is to that boundary that we now turn our attention.

The difference between being humbled and humiliated is a crucial one. We are humbled when we discover in a more profound sense who we really are. To be humbled is to have some illusions and delusions shattered, to be sure, and so it can be painful and even traumatic. But it is a good process because it involves the removal of the false self. Humiliation, on the other hand, is an attack on the true self. It can come in several forms. The most toxic sort is a result of the intentional actions of another. Inflicted or intentional humiliation is what happens when someone goes out of their way to belittle, demean or denigrate us. We all know what it is like to feel on the wrong end of inflicted or intentional humiliation. We feel the power of the other and discover our helplessness in the face of it. All bullying is a form of inflicted humiliation and so too is sexual or racial harassment. We are today very alert to the negative consequences of such humiliation and rightly see that there are issues of justice at stake when we engage in or collude with such behaviour.

Second, there is moral humiliation. This is the humiliation that comes when we realize that we have been *overestimating* our intellectual, physical or moral capabilities. Moral humiliation is the fall that comes after pride and which can help us grow in humility. It is good for us to be humbled in this way because it exposes our arrogance. We will consider the nature of pride shortly, but at this stage the important point is that an experience of good humiliation is one that alerts us to an aspect of ourselves, a type of behaviour, a habit or an attitude which does not speak of personal humility but of its opposite. Such humiliation can be an entirely personal and private matter. No one else need ever know. If we notice it and reflect profoundly on it so that we can learn its lessons, moral humiliation can lead to some personal enlightenment.

Whereas moral humiliation is something we should take to heart and learn from, inflicted humiliation, which comes from being bullied or abused, should provoke in us not soul-searching but anger. I know that real life is not always that straightforward, but it is important for us to distinguish with all the wisdom we can muster whether we are in a situation that calls out primarily for justice or whether we are in a situation which calls out for our own repentance. We endanger ourselves if we take too polarized a view of this. The Christian tendency used to be to take the blame and to respond to humiliation with repentance and sorrow – assuming it to have been my fault. That approach is not so prevalent today. There are more 'Teflon' people to whom no blame can ever stick in today's BSE (Blame Someone Else) society. It is more common than ever to come across people with the sort of sloping shoulders on which no responsibility can rest. The reality is that our response to humiliation needs to be open and wise whenever it occurs. Sometimes we must be candid and say that, 'Much as I know that I can be a problem and a pain myself, and that I do make real mistakes and errors of judgement, there are times when I am indeed more sinned against than sinning. That does not make me a good person but it might mean that what is primarily required of me now is a passion for justice.' On other occasions we might say something very different, 'Come to think of it, on reflection, and when you put it like that, I do have to take responsibility for some of the mess we find ourselves in now. Part of this is just something to do with who I am, my habitual capacity to put my foot in it. But thinking back I recognize that I should have planned things more carefully or responded with more tact. Yes, this has taken me down a peg or two, but fair enough. I take my share of the blame and sanction and will seek to do better in the future.' Personally I very much prefer having to make the first of these two speeches. However, as Barefoot Disciples and people of passionate humility, we need to find the wisdom and courage to be able to make either speech as appropriate. In the one we are looking for justice. In the other we are looking for forgiveness. Both are good and there is no shame in seeking either. If an act of humiliation sets us off on either journey, it will have had a good outcome.

Good Pride

If we modern people are far more reluctant to accept blame than were our forebears, then we are also less inclined to castigate pride. There are good and not so good sides to that. For medieval theologians such as Thomas Aquinas, pride was 'the queen of sins' representing 'an excessive love of one's own excellence'; a view which goes back at least as far as St Augustine. Today we are more indulgent of ourselves and others. Impressed by the rise of science since the Enlightenment, and an awareness of the psychological corrosiveness of negative thinking, modern people tend to be a bit more inclined to feel that pride is a good thing. There is truth on both the ancient and modern sides of the argument because there is more than one kind of pride. There is both 'sinful pride' and 'good pride'. The important thing for us to recognize, perhaps, is that the existence and importance of one does not contradict the existence or importance of the other.

Good pride is seen in the first chapter of the book of Genesis, where, at the end of each day, God looks over his work of creating and recognizes that it is 'very good'. This is the sort of pride that we should allow ourselves to experience. There is no reason for human beings not to feel good about work well done, about sound or surprising achievements. It is right to have a realistic and positive pride in what we have actually done. There is no reason why we should not only notice, but also delight in, our personal achievements. To illustrate this I am going to risk sharing some of my own personal pride. My intention here is not to persuade you to admire my achievement (it is more likely that it will make you smile) but that in reading about it you will feel encouraged to feel a good pride in something you have done, achieved or learnt.

It was in my forties that I first picked up a saxophone and had a hopeful blow. My arrogant assumption was that I should be able to do this quite easily. No sound came out of the other end at first, but suddenly there was a loud and rude blast. The word 'burp' comes to mind. Five years later I had passed a number of exams and was playing with others, sometimes in public. I feel very proud about that, even if in a slightly amused and lighthearted sort of way. Sadly, I discovered no hidden musical genius in myself, in fact I discovered that for me rehearsing and remembering scales is immensely difficult. The experience of the learning, which involved going to classes and seeing children learn faster, was of being humbled, as was sight-reading in exams; I cringe to think about it. The result, however, was a growth in confidence which I can relate with pride because I am sure that none of this makes me any better than anyone else. I am sure that I am at least as prone to conceit as other people but I don't *feel* that this adult learning experience, or telling the story of it, has made me conceited. Indeed, the process has, if anything, caused me to admire others all the more. As human beings we can grow in the capacity to appreciate others only if we are able to accept that we too have achieved the occasional thing of value. If God can say at the end of each of the six mythical days of creation that the results are 'very good' there is no reason why we should not at least smile and say, 'Not bad' when we notice that we or others have done something worthwhile or fulfilling, especially if what we have learnt in the process is not how special we are but how special others are.

The reality is that adult learning can be profoundly humbling. Learning a new skill in adult years confronts us with what we find difficult. This is perhaps why the sight of adults learning is so moving and encouraging. I still recall seeing my scout master struggling to learn how to swim when I was a teenager. He would be panting away at widths while the rest of us were diving and swimming lengths in different strokes and under water. Then there are those who pass their driving test after several failures and who at one stage could not tell left from right. One of the privileges of my current post is to speak at diocesan lay education courses and to share in the 'graduation' services at the end of the year. The sense of new confidence and good pride is itself a delight which is often shared not only by the beaming graduates, but also by their happy supporters. Such delight, while based in a way on personal achievement, is a social joy to the extent to which it is not tainted by arrogance or conceit. The ideal on such occasions is that everyone is special and no one is superior. To the degree to which this is realized, they are intimations of the kingdom of God.

For most of us, the down-to-earth reality is that we are special in this ordinary way and ordinary in a special way. Delighting in such special ordinariness, however, is a primary pleasure of the humble. Humility has an eye, an ear, a mind and a heart for the delightful, wherever it is to be found. And if it finds it close to home, it will know that this is not because of the absence of mistakes or an unusual ease of learning. Rather it will simply be because home is the place where we spend most time and we are the person of whom we have most knowledge. It is not arrogant or conceited to delight in your own achievements. That fault only arises if you think that those achievements make you better or more important or valuable than the next person. They don't. To follow Jesus we need to get over ourselves. We are, however, so deeply ego-centric and complicated that this will take quite a long time and a lot of help. To seek to develop patience and to begin to ask for help are early steps on the journey to humility.

That we need to be able to distinguish between good and bad pride first occurred to me when it was my task to lead a restoration project for an ancient parish church and we chose as our first priority 'to restore pride in the town's historic parish church'. It was important for us to name this task. The congregation was demoralized and daunted by the scale of the challenge. Water was dripping through the roof and soaking through ancient stone, broken windows were left broken, litter remained uncollected in the churchyard and, as evidence of vandalism accumulated, so it attracted more. The only thing flourishing was a big fruiting

fungus: *serpula lacrymans* – dry rot. Signs of pride were conspic-
uously absent. But this was *not* a good thing. It was, in fact, a
failure to value the inheritance of the past and to imagine the way
in which this Grade 1 listed building could speak to the present
and serve the future. Although it had never been named as such,
the work of restoring pride had actually started well before I
arrived, with the restoration of the church tower. Indeed, that
project generated a considerable amount of pride in the achievement, the bells ringing out again after several years of silence being
a great sign of triumph. What this did not prepare the parishioners
for, however, was how to cope with the disappointment which
came when, no sooner had that great task been achieved, a rather
less glamorous and more intractable one became necessary at the
other end of the church building.

The task of restoring a church is an apt metaphor for restoring
pride. Both are long tasks, taking decades rather than months,
involving much hard and often unseen work and always remaining
a work in progress. And both can stand as metaphors for redemp-
tion. It is a process from death to life, from suffering to victory,
from cross to resurrection.

Good pride and healthy or passionate humility really do
belong together in the attitudes and values of Jesus' apprentices,
the Barefoot Disciples. It is right for us to have a form of pride
in who we are and what we have done. It is good for us to have
enough confidence to live with dignity, relish enjoyment and be
able to offer service, welcome and hospitality to others. Satisfaction is not the same thing as smugness, and there is a degree
of emotional honesty when we look at our work with warm
pride. Indeed, pride in this sense is both essential and inevitable
in a healthy personality. This sort of pride need not be corrosive
of humility. In fact, healthy pride feeds the very confidence that
is integral to the process of learning humility, becoming humble.

Bad Pride

Not all pride is good, however. There is also bad pride: pride the sin or hubris. This is pride that has got out of hand and gone to the head. All too often this leads to boasting, as Bernard of Clairvaux observed in his monastery. We may not know many monks, but we probably recognize this fellow, possibly in ourselves.

> He is full of words and the swelling spirit strains within him. His hunger and thirst are for listeners, someone to listen to his boasting, on whom he can pour out all his thoughts, someone he can show what a big man he is. At last the chance to speak comes. The discussion turns on literature. He brings forth from his treasury things old and new. He is not shy about producing his opinions; words are bubbling over. He does not wait to be asked. His information comes before any question. He asks the questions; gives the answers; cuts off anyone who tries to speak. When the bell rings and it is necessary to interrupt the conversation, hour-long though it be, he seeks a minute more. He must get special permission to resume his talk, not to edify his listeners, but to show off his learning. He may have the capacity to help others but that is the least of his concerns. His aim is not to teach you nor to be taught by you, but to show how much he knows.[1]

The philosopher Gabriele Taylor offers an analysis of bad pride in her book *Pride, Shame and Guilt*.[2] Helpfully she distinguishes between arrogance and conceit. The arrogant are those who take their superiority to others absolutely for granted. Taylor suggests we think of Mr Darcy in *Pride and Prejudice*. The conceited, on the other hand, are those who believe that they have earned their superior position. Taylor suggests we think of Mr Bounderby in *Hard Times*. Unlike the complacent and aloof Darcy, Bounderby is 'conceited, vain and boastful'.[3] But both are a long way from humility, passionate or otherwise.

Conceit is annoying and socially corrosive but it is not as bad as arrogance. Arrogance involves an excessive sense of superiority and self-importance, and is sometimes coupled with the denigration, fear and envy of others. Arrogance is the pitiable form of our self-regard when we are at our most self-deluding. And there can be no good, beautiful or healthy form of arrogance. While proud humility is a rich and healthy paradox, humble arrogance is an oxymoron, a contradiction in terms. The failures of arrogance are all too predictable. They come from the proud refusal to consider carefully whether a project has a realistic chance of success. This is the Luke 14 scenario that we saw in Chapter 1: the man building a tower or waging a campaign without reckoning on how costly it will be. This is the sort of thing that happens when we are filled with bravado and over-confidence: the 'I can do it' attitude which emphasizes the 'I'. The irony is that when we are acting out of arrogance, we experience failure as debilitating humiliation. When we fall from arrogance, we do not know what to do next. The drama we envisaged has gone wrong. There is nothing that can be done, no Plan B. Like the primordial couple in the Garden of Eden, we want to hide away and cover our shame. Most tragically of all, the opportunity to learn, which is what all failure and mistake-making brings, is lost.

Although good pride is connected with both humility and confidence, the relationship between arrogance and confidence is tenser. Arrogance can come out when our confidence is either inappropriately high, or when it has deserted us altogether. We can exude confidence both when we are highly competent and when we are trying to cover up our feelings of inadequacy. Maybe we should think in terms of 'appropriate confidence'. That is, the kind of confidence which is based on an honest appraisal of our personal limits and potential and which is formed in awareness of the fact that we have made mistakes and that we will make plenty more in the future.

Arrogance is a serious, possibly even malignant, mistake for a disciple. First, because it is difficult if not impossible to learn once arrogance sets in. Second, because when human beings lose the capacity to learn, it is just a matter of time before humiliation arrives. The Greek myth of Icarus is the most spectacular example of a fall from arrogance. Icarus' father Daedalus had perfected the art of making wings from feathers and wax. Icarus loved the sensation of flying and forgot his father's warning not to fly too close to the sun. When he made his mistake the wax melted, the wings failed and he fell into the sea. In terms of the distinctions we are forming here, it is *arrogance* that comes before a fall. It is arrogance, not passion or good pride, that both leads to our humiliation and prevents us from recovering.

Jesus repeatedly warned against arrogance. The Pharisee who thanked God that he was 'not like other men' was judged harshly, while the tax collector who sought mercy as a sinner 'went home justified' (Luke 18.9–14). For some reason, we invariably find the errors and mistakes of others to be far more obvious and important than our own. We might laugh when someone tells us the joke about a Sunday School teacher who said to the children after they had been read that story, 'and now let us give thanks to God that we are not like that awful Pharisee'. But the point is that sometimes, at least, we are very much like that awful Pharisee (or, for that matter, that silly Sunday School teacher). We easily fall into judgemental mode and notice the speck in our brother's or sister's eye while failing to notice the beam in our own (Luke 6.42). But other people do not exist to make us feel better about ourselves. Other people are there for the same reason as us, which is to reflect divine glory by participating in God's mission, walking the Christlike way and being open to God's Spirit. To believe this is to hold Christian faith. To live it with passionate humility is the calling of the Barefoot Disciple.

A different pathology applies when we are at the other end of the spectrum of self-delusion. Not the arrogance end, but the end of grovelling lowliness, for which I will use the word 'abject'. When we are feeling abject, we do not assume that because things depend on us, they will work out well. Rather, we expect our efforts to result in failure. The French philosopher Simone Weil resisted baptism in part because she experienced a 'general sense of inadequacy'. Although she could not transcend this she was wise enough to know that it was not the same thing as genuine humility. '[I]f I possessed the virtue of humility, the most beautiful of all virtues perhaps, I should not be in this miserable state of inadequacy.'⁴ She is right about this and the point needs to be underlined. Humility is not inadequacy or abjectness. Indeed, the presence of abjectness is evidence that we are a long way from humility. We will never grovel our way either to fullness of life or to the kingdom of God.

The pathology of abjectness is quite different from the pathology of arrogance. When we feel abject or inadequate we are inclined to set our sights low and aim to underachieve. While the arrogant fear failure, the lowly fear success. Worse than this, the lowly fear being perceived as those who think that they might actually achieve something. They are frightened of being seen to be standing in a position from which it is possible to fall. It's the shame of being seen to be thinking too highly of oneself. This is very common, not least in the Church. But it is not healthy. Sometimes we will fail because we are over-confident, other times we will fail because we are under-confident. What is without doubt is that *we will fail*. This is the grain of truth, the priceless pearl of self-awareness, that the Barefoot Disciple, the person of passionate humility, carries in their heart. If Aristotle had considered humility to be a virtue, maybe it would have been at the 'golden mean' between the two extremes of abjectness and arrogance.

Rhetorical Humility

One of the entries I most enjoyed writing in my journal of a sabbatical visit to South Africa described my experiences when visiting a very small chapel in a desolate area of the Cape Flats. I will say much more about this visit in Chapter 5, but for now I want to record that I was surprised to read at the end of my account that I had used the cliché, 'It was very humbling'. I have often wondered exactly what we mean by this phrase, being slightly concerned that there might be something at least paradoxical, if not ironic, in ascribing to oneself an increase in humility. But I have come to realize that the phrase does not really mean, 'I think I am more humble now'. Rather, people use it to attest that they have been surprised by the virtue or strength of character or the capacity to cope with adversity of another. To say that you 'feel humbled' is to experience an unexpected surge of respect for what another person has suffered and survived or achieved against the odds. It means that the speaker (or writer) realizes that another's experience has put their own into fresh perspective. It is the deep learning that such occasions facilitate that authenticates as genuine humility. We are humbled when we learn one of life's great, deep, simple lessons by observing the lives of others. Adult learning is humbling both because it happens and also because we are so aware of the pain that we experience in the process and of the painful pace of our own development. We are humbled when we see children effortlessly absorbing information that just won't lodge in our minds, or acquiring skills that seem to elude us no matter how hard we practise.

That's part of it, but there is yet more to 'feeling humbled'. Sometimes we talk of being humbled when we mean that we are proud in a good sense but don't want to use that word because we are all too aware that it can be used in a bad sense. We talk of 'being humbled' when we have done well in order to express pride without being duped into conceit ourselves, or seeming to have become conceited to others. Such 'rhetorical humility' is sometimes used by those who can admit to feeling pride in their talents and achievements but do not want to lose their sense of being part of the wider community and fellowship of ordinary people. It is a trope of exceptional people who know that they are exceptional but who do not want to feel disconnected or identified as too different and therefore 'out of touch'. In this way, the phrase is a way of saying 'I am honoured', in a culture where the word 'honour' seems too archaic.

This is the kind of humility that Barack Obama voiced in his speech accepting the democratic nomination for President of the United States in August 2008. 'With profound gratitude and great humility, I accept your nomination for the presidency of the United States.' This sort of rhetorical humility conveys the message that the speaker, singled out for honour or office and thus recognized as, or rendered, exceptional, still sees himself as a person like all others. Indeed, Obama devoted the first few minutes of his speech to making connections with other key individuals. First, he mentioned his opponent and then recent Democratic Presidents. Next, he named his nuclear family (of whom he affirmed that he was proud) before referring to his own story and ancestry. These paragraphs filled out the meaning of the word 'humility' in his opening sentence. It meant: this is the sort of person I am, this is the sort of company I keep, such are my ancestors and peers. Rhetorical humility is proud humility. Rhetorical humility dares, indeed needs, to speak its own name surprisingly often and yet does so in a way which, unlike Uriah Heap's ''umble humility', *does* have integrity. Rhetorical humility says, 'I may have a new status or a special assignment, I have indeed been singled out, but I am still a person of flesh and blood like you. There is more continuity than discontinuity here. I am still *me*. I remain still one of you.'

Rhetorical humility is, at one level, a plea to be seen as a real person despite being exceptional, normal despite being different. But it also has a note of promise about it. 'Yes, I can see and feel the honour of my position, but I am determined not to let it go to my head.' These are worthy sentiments. But the hearer knows that they are only hopes and promises. The experience of being humbled, when we observe or hear of someone such as Rena Canipe (see Chapter 1), is a genuine learning experience: we *are* changed. Rhetorical humility, on the other hand, is a promise *not* to be changed by fame and fortune, position or wealth.

It follows that while rhetorical humility is not quite the real thing, it is not necessarily to be sneered at. Certainly it is inadequate to think of humility as the capacity to summon up a modest response to personal success, or to fain surprise when ambition is rewarded. Sincere, attitudinal humility is not concerned with impression at all. The genuinely humble do not mind if they are seen to be above themselves, for they do not calibrate communities in terms of status. The concern of the genuinely humble is to be real, direct and truthful. Rhetorical humility may sometimes be a bit hard to hear without a wry smile, but it does have something to teach us. For not all pride is vain, arrogant or sinful. Some pride, like some humility, is real, good and appropriate. And it is where these overlap that humility sometimes dares to speak its own name.

In contrast to rhetorical humility stands false modesty, which is far more complex and potentially manipulative than we might at first realize. It too can be rhetorical. And it too can be used to cover its own tracks and disguise a cruel arrogance or haughtiness. A satirical guide book to help the French survive the English, *Le Dossier*, puts it like this:

A large part of the famous English humour – allied to 'not taking yourself too seriously' – consists in undermining one's own achievements, which is very wearisome. I was sitting next to a prize-winning professor once, who told me that he 'fiddled around in a lab' for a living. This false modesty is considered most amusing, and the joke is on you when you later discover he is in fact the cleverest man in the world. I call it dishonest and bad manners.[5]

When, later in the book, the author offers 'Ten reasons to hate the English' she has as the third point: 'Their false modesty. In reality the English are viciously competitive'.[6] The Abbot of Worth picks up on the same word when he explains the Benedictine approach to humility. He says that without the integrity and consistency between what is said and what is felt, modesty is, as he found it described in a Victorian guide to good manners, 'vicious'. The guide deprecates sentences which begin with phrases like 'Well, of course I am not expert, but it seems to me ...' or 'Ignorant as I am, I hesitate to express an opinion ...' The abbot comments:

> These opening phrases are 'vicious' because they are false humility; as Benedict puts it, the speaker 'only admits with the tongue.' If the speaker really believed his opening gambit, he would keep silent. What the speaker is doing, paradoxically, is gaining your approval for his opinion; by pretending it is worthless, he hopes you will affirm that the opinion is in fact correct with a 'Come, come, sir, you do yourself an injustice; that is a sound opinion.'[7]

Those who call false modesty 'vicious' are making the point that it is the opposite of a virtue; in other words, it is a vice. A genuinely humble person will not engage in false modesty because it is dishonest. Humility involves openness to the truth, and humble people are open about the truth, usually in a very straightforward way. False modesty is the hypocritical behaviour of the 'wolves in sheep's clothing' whom Jesus warns us about in the Sermon on the Mount (Matthew 7.15). We need to be alert to this tendency both in others and in ourselves.

Nonetheless, there is something profoundly winning and good about those who are all too aware that they might be giving an impression of themselves that is better than the reality of whom they are – that they are not quite as special as the pedestal on which they stand suggests. Sometimes it is right to use 'rhetorical humility' to try to get this point across. It is not the same as false modesty, and while in our culture it is easy to mock, humility requires of us that we give the recently honoured, who speak of being humbled, at least some benefit of the doubt.

Notes

1. Bernard of Clairvaux, *The Steps of Humility and Pride*, p. 69.
2. Taylor, *Pride, Shame, and Guilt*, p. 48.
3. Taylor, *Pride, Shame, and Guilt*, p. 49.
4. Weil, *Waiting on God*, p. 3.
5. Long, *Le Dossier*, p. 32.
6. Long, *Le Dossier*, p. 258.
7. Jamison, *Finding Sanctuary*, p. 105.

CHAPTER 5

Childlike Maturity

God Loves Adults Too

People were bringing the children for Jesus to touch and bless. But the disciples were dead against it, indeed they 'sternly ordered them not to do it' (Luke 18.15). It takes a moment to take this on board. They did not invite them to desist, nor did they suggest a distraction. Neither did they say, 'Let us do the blessing while Jesus does the teaching.' They did not merely ask them or tell them not to do this. They *ordered them sternly*. The language here is of power, and power wielded harshly. But Jesus is having none of it. 'Let the children come to me,' he says, 'it is to such as these that the kingdom of God belongs' (Luke 18.16). What on earth did he mean?

In his scholarly book, *Adults as Children*, James Francis argues that for Jesus, childhood was a vital metaphor for discipleship, that Jesus was saying something very odd (metaphorical) when he was saying that Jesus' disciples, those who seek God's kingdom, should be *as children*.[1] When Jesus says that we should be 'as little children' he is saying that Christian adults are those whose identity and character have been renewed as children of God. Taking the New Testament as a whole, he reveals, and this is the point of such books, just how complicated this apparently simple matter is. But this should not surprise us. The best known passage in Paul's writing has this sentence at its heart: 'When I was a child, I spoke like a child, I thought like a child, I reasoned like a child; when I became an adult, I put an end to childish ways' (1 Corinthians 13.11). This, of course, is the opposite of Jesus' approach. We might reasonably expect Jesus to have said something more like this: 'As I become an adult so I also become, paradoxically and strangely, even more like a child. True maturity is about learning how to be a child.' As Bruno Schulz put it, 'My ideal would be to "mature" into childhood. That would be genuine maturity.'

There is truth in both. Jesus' focus is on the childlikeness that is integral to Christian maturity. Paul's is on the childishness that is to be left behind as we mature in faith. Preachers often remind people of this and tell them in practical terms what *childlikeness* is and encourage them in it, and at the same time seek to clarify what *childishness* is and dissuade them from it. We can perhaps name some of the qualities that Jesus was hoping we would understand and acquire by talking as he does of the need for adults to be 'as children'. Among these, the qualities of being trusting and humble appear again and again in Francis' book: these are the qualities that come to the surface when adults know that they are children of God. The point is that Christian humility is not a matter of adults living out the characteristics of babies, infants or children. Christian humility is found in a personality reshaped and renewed by relationship with God. What makes Christian humility radical is not its immaturity but the quality of its maturity. Whether we call this childlikeness or Christlikeness matters little. What is at stake is the vision of maturity.

Christian maturity must always be marked by qualities such as 'trust' and 'humility' which are far from the top of our culture's hierarchy of values. Not many students go to university with the ambition of becoming more trusting and humble. Once again, we see just how the Christian vision of maturity is at odds with our 'normal' expectations and assumptions today. Which perhaps means that we should think more deeply about what Jesus might mean by saying that the kingdom of God is entered by those who are 'as children'.

When it comes to our attitude towards maturity, we tend to line up all too easily alongside not Jesus but his sternly-ordering disciples, and we see this played out in our attitude to children. Our fault is not that we overtly seek to exclude. We act with more subtlety than that. But in a world where power is unevenly distributed, and it always is, what we mean by 'child' is a person or type of person who is closer to the powerless, dependent, permission-needing end of the spectrum. We only need to change the idiom slightly to realize that these are 'the poor'. At the other end of the spectrum, we find the people of status and influence, the permission-givers, the gatekeepers, most of whom characteristically deny that they hold any real power because power always seeks to disguise itself. In a word, we find 'the rich'. Wealth and power seek to exclude the truly childlike, whether it is found in a real live infant or in a genuinely humble Christian adult.

Churches today often have worried discussions about children as members and participants. There is a lot of anxiety, a certain amount of self-righteousness and, I suspect, a good measure of unhealed memory in this discussion. This means that it is often somewhat heated and in danger of being unnecessarily polarized. One group feel that the imperative is to have children in church so that it can be a wholesome and inclusive church today, while the other group want to prioritize children so that the Church will have a better chance of surviving into the future. While they are both reasonable and potentially overlapping points of view, neither does justice to the truth Jesus was trying to communicate by his teaching about and with children.

The litmus test of a church is not the presence or absence of children, but the kind of maturity that the adults show; for it is Christian *adults* who are to be 'as children'. If that maturity is based on status and importance, on power and position, prestige and privilege, then it is only, in Christian terms, quasi-maturity, apparent maturity. But if it is childlike maturity, then we are surely along the right lines, and the question of the presence of children will take care of itself. For it is adults with true, Christian, childlike maturity among whom young children feel relaxed, at home and welcome. It is Christian adults who, on beholding each other, see not a person of status, or a figure of fun or fear, or even a hated enemy, but a child of God, and can relate easily with children and adults alike. We know that Jesus loves children. The surprising, challenging news for most of us is that God loves adults, because compared with loving children, loving adults can be really quite difficult. Why? Because all too often life unfolds in such a way as to hurt people so deeply that they never bounce back. Life is harmful. It inflicts wounds. Life, you could say, damages your health, certainly your physical health, but all too often there is psychological and spiritual damage too.

Natural Humiliation

In the previous chapter we reflected on the difference between inflicted humiliation and moral humiliation. Now we turn to 'natural humiliation', humiliation that occurs when, for whatever reasons, our capacities are diminished or less than we would like them to be. Age, illness or accident can bring this on quickly or slowly and it can be very difficult for people to accept. We often experience such humiliation as shame or embarrassment. We are aware of letting others down, or appearing to their gaze as less than we would like to be. There is painful self-awareness in this experience and we often shy away from it, hiding our distress and humiliation. People often try to cover up disorders and disabilities because they feel that others will regard them with less respect if they are revealed. There are cultural sensitivities in this. People of an older generation will avoid at all costs letting you discover their illiteracy or clumsiness, whereas modern parents will encourage their children to be very up-front about their dyslexia or dyspraxia. Different losses of capacity are differently embarrassing. Thus today the need for glasses carries no shame or embarrassment. However, it was not so a couple of generations ago. Myopic children were taunted as 'four eyes' and some still live with the emotional scars in their senior years. Strangely, hearing loss is more shaming than loss of visual acuity: people are more reluctant to wear hearing aids than spectacles. The onset of the loss of hair or memory are seen as embarrassing and people try to cover up both for as long as they can, combing wispy threads over their forgetful crowns. Those who suffer from migraine, which is not age-related, often find that an attack comes with a significant drop in self-esteem and so they simultaneously feel bad about themselves and in pain because of the migraine and yet try to cover up or deny the condition. This is unfortunate as the condition itself can lead to impaired performance on simple tasks and a difficulty in listening to others or absorbing new information. I have struggled through meetings, sermons and funerals with a migraine: feeling bad, looking worse but not yet confident enough to explain what is going on in me. It is not always easy or appropriate to do so, but the point remains that 'natural humiliation' can be a chronic or episodic feature of life for many, if not all of us. True humility, however, is found in accepting who we really are. As Paul writes in his letter to the Romans: 'For by the grace given to me I say to everyone among you not to think of yourself more highly than you ought to think, but to think with sober judgement, each according to the measure of faith that God has assigned' (Romans 12.3). True humility involves coming to terms with natural humiliation.

Much natural humiliation comes though the process of ageing. Generally speaking, we are relaxed about dyeing our hair to give the impression that we are younger than our years. We do not see it as a moral issue. I wonder, however. What about solidarity with the 'grey community'? The association of greyness with age is ancient and biblical: Psalm 71.18 puts the two together 'even to old age and grey hairs'. The same connection is made in Isaiah 46.4. In both cases grey means old, and old means to have lost ability and become dependent and vulnerable. Dependence and vulnerability are seen as unattractive and undesirable traits. So much so that we feel that the possibility of venerability, wisdom, distinction or entitlement to respect that comes with age and its marker, grey hair, is worth forfeiting if one can give the impression of unnatural youth and vigour.

To return to deeper matters, diminishing physical and mental capacities *are* humiliating. We saw this earlier with the story of Rena Canipe (Chapter 1) but it is a familiar one not only to those inflicted with Alzheimer's, but a myriad of the consequences of having lived beyond our prime. Diminishing capacities are sure to humiliate us but will not necessarily humble us. For one thing, it is not necessarily good or healthy to expect less of ourselves than we might have previously reasonably accepted. Part of health – intellectual, physical and moral – depends on responding with a little more effort after disappointment. This is perhaps what makes the onset of a disease like Alzheimer's so difficult. On the one hand our only choice is to accept, on the other hand we must resist in order to stave off the symptoms and maintain our diminishing faculties as long as possible. There is no point in rushing into dependency. Worthington is right to identify this phase of life at which the presence or absence of key virtues makes a major difference. He focused on his mother-in-law's humility, but he might also have identified her courage and wisdom.

Pessimism and Play

Arthur Schopenhauer, writing in the early nineteenth century, was an eloquent preacher of pessimism. He is the original grumpy old man. His view of ageing was that 'it is bad today, and it will be worse tomorrow and so on till the worst of all'. This vision of perpetual decline from childhood to age and death is not so very far from the way many of us think today. Life has a tremendous capacity to disappoint. Schopenhauer puts it like this in his essay 'On the Suffering of the World':

> If two men who were friends in their youth meet again when they are old, after being separated for a life-time, the chief feeling they will have at the sight of each other will be one of complete disappointment at life as a whole; because their thoughts will be carried back to that earlier time when life seemed so fair as it lay spread out before them in the rosy light of dawn, promised so much – and then performed so little. This feeling will so completely predominate over every other that they will not even consider it necessary to give it words; but on either side it will be silently assumed, and the ground work of all that they have to talk about.[2]

I once quoted in a sermon Schopenhauer's view that older people are necessarily disappointed. It did not go down at all well among the senior members of the congregation. Afterwards they accused me of 'getting at them'. Part of me thought that, like Lady Macbeth, they 'doth protest too much'. But part of me had to recognize that many had suffered in all sorts of ways throughout their lives. A typical example would involve the experience of war, poverty, personal illness and close bereavement. What was startling was that they had come through it all so positively, that they had somehow managed to weather these storms and come through smiling. If *they* were to meet someone they had not seen for years, and I witnessed such reunions from time to time, the tone did not seem to be shared disappointment so much as rekindled youthfulness. Those were the days, indeed. Unlike Schopenhauer's disappointed and grumpy old people, these people were still awake and alert to the possibility that life could be a delight.

Such people are a testimony to our capacity for what one might call 'retrospective optimism'. That is, to forget the pain of some of life's more difficult times and to remember the things that delight. Not that the memory can be entirely left to its own devices in this regard. There are plenty of people who would echo or mirror Schopenhauer's miserable pessimism. They may not readily form a club or be prominent in a fellowship, indeed the sadness of their condition is that pessimism is isolating. It aggravates loneliness. Those who expect the worst are not given any joy when it happens because there is, in fact, no antidote for disappointment. Like so many of life's more difficult blessings, it needs to be embraced, experienced and learnt from. We can only ever expect to transcend our disappointments if we allow ourselves to really feel them. To help myself cope with disappointment, I have sometimes used the image of a squash ball on impact with the wall of the court to describe the experience. The wise thing, it seems to me, is not to deny that the wall feels hard or that the ball is almost flattened, rather it is to accept the process, realize that hopes and aspirations have all too suddenly come to a halt and to hold the moment carefully, so that most of the energy of impact will become the energy with which one moves off in a different direction.

It might be that our passion causes us to have a disappointing collision with an immovable obstacle, but it is our humility which allows us to regroup, reorient and re-gather our energy and purpose. Humility does not mean hitting the wall like a jelly. Passionate humility involves the realism of the squash ball. Yes, we are more or less flattened. No, we do not dribble down the wall into a heap. Every disappointment is a blessing in disguise and we will only see it for what it is when we realize that it is a learning opportunity. The challenge is to learn from the impact, accept the pain, give thanks for the lesson and set off again. I know that this is far easier said than done. But it is a process to which the outlook and attitudes of so many elderly people attest. These are the ones who have learnt how to count their blessings and give thanks for the past. Old age does not come alone, they say, but if the process of growing up and growing old has rendered people sad and disillusioned, disappointed and embittered, we cannot say that they have attained true maturity, no matter how grey the hair or wrinkled the skin. A more childlike maturity involves working with the grain of retrospective optimism and feeding it with simple and humble practices like counting your blessings and being thankful. It may sound patronizing to say that we have to accept our disappointments, but maybe it is more childlike to learn from them than to rail against them, even if they do flatten us out for a while.

A central question for any Christian disciple is what happens to the 'child within' as the years go by. If that child is carefully nurtured, it will grow and flourish. If it is neglected, it will shrivel and shrink in diminishment and disappointment. Part of the work of Christian discipleship must therefore be to nourish and encourage, to strengthen and support, the inner child. Only by giving it some proper attention can growing and ageing adult disciples expect to become more open and trusting as they go through the ups and downs of life. Authentic Christian discipleship must always include the things that children thrive on: opportunities to play, to learn, to make a mess, to enjoy food and drink, to be emotionally expressive and to show unconditional respect to elders.

The truth of this came home to me in a profound way when I was involved in an ecumenical project to support refugees and asylum seekers. It was not at all clear what we could or should do. Certainly there were collections of basic kitchen utensils and clothes to help them, but in the end we decided to focus our efforts on helping the children to play. It is always difficult to know how successful such activities are, but it seemed to me that if the criterion of success was in helping all concerned to recognize each other's common humanity, then it has worked well. If people passed some time together creatively, joyfully and delightfully, it was a triumph. It is hard to maintain the barriers which are inevitably created when we engage in charitable or philanthropic efforts when the object of the exercise is to have fun together. And at the end of the day, or indeed at the end of all days, it might be that the capacity to play is the aspect of our humanity that stands us in the best stead for what is to come. When I was a theology student I was given an essay title which has proved to me more memorable than most: 'If there is no sex in heaven, what is the point of the resurrection of the body?' The context of this was a recent Papal Encyclical which had gone out of its way to make this rather negative point. The correct answer, if I now recall the answer as well as the question, was something to do with identity and communication. But it strikes me that an answer which referred to play as the pastime of eternity might not be a bad one. If there is no play in heaven, no playfulness, no timeless delighting in things for their own sake, then eternity could seem like a very long time indeed. It is a good instinct that gives angels musical instruments to play, and which expects us to sing. For however much skill is involved, these are very child-like ways to pass the time.

One of the best things that happened during my tenure as a parish priest was that we set up an 'all age orchestra' to accompany the hymns at one service a month. It was an 'all ability' effort too, which meant that I could join in because I was at that stage learning the recorder alongside my kids, something I had got stuck with after note 'G' when at school. Somehow the organist, conducting from the electric piano, held it all together. As time went by, so people got old instruments out of the attic, dusted them down and started to play again. Friends were brought to church to help out and ended up joining in more deeply than they had expected. Some Sundays there were rather strange ensembles: five recorders, two bassoons and a guitar; two violins, a piano accordion, three cellos, a saxophone and a guitar. The children, of course, put the adults to shame by progressing more quickly, but the adults taught the children some of the disciplines of participation. I enjoyed not only taking part myself but also the way in which playing in the orchestra got people to church early to set up and practise, and this, in turn, encouraged others to be in good time. The place became friendlier and more hospitable. It was not long before the question was raised about what to play at the end of the service. We could hardly just stop, and yet trying to play typical recessional music would have been a joke. The answer was to play the kind of music that the congregation would enjoy hearing. This ranged from Music Hall favourites to songs from the shows and melodious Beatles numbers like 'Yesterday'. On Christmas Eve we played 'White Christmas', and when the bishop came he processed out to the 'Lambeth Walk', the whole, smiling congregation joining in with the 'Oi'. Call me a heretic but I think there was more joy, both in church, and in heaven, over those 'Oi's than over 99 organ voluntaries during which everyone rushes for the door before the place is quiet enough for a conversation. These 'secular' pieces never detracted from the worship but they always added enormously to the atmosphere and happiness of the gathering.

The Lord, He Knows Best

One of the occasions that had the biggest impact on me during a sabbatical visit to South Africa was spending a couple of days with people I will call Amos and Martha in their home on the Cape Flats. Martha explained to me that she and Amos had nine children and eight grandchildren. However, this did not begin to describe their household, which included all sorts of relations and neighbours who shared some of their space some of the time. Some of these people have their own homes elsewhere, some stay for a night or two at a time. Indeed, I could not tell how many people stayed there on my two nights. The small shed outside was euphemistically called 'the bungalow' and seemed to provide several people with a place to stay.

Amos and Martha had set up what they call a 'shanty church' on the dunes in a particularly impoverished area. The church building was a corrugated iron structure, a shack among the shacks. They took me to see it on a day when they were running a soup kitchen for the children of the area. Although people were glad that I was there, they were also slightly embarrassed. There was not quite as much soup as usual, and there were no clothes to give away. Amos noticed that people were concerned that I would not see the project on a particularly good day and commented, 'The Lord, he knows best.' And, indeed, when the saucepan lid was bashed with the wooden spoon, fewer people than usual came along. Those who did were children or teenagers. Most of them carried empty margarine tubs to contain their portion of soup made with meat and white corn (mealie). It was not the sort of thing that I have ever seen young people queuing up for before. As they waited patiently for it to be served, we were all given a small tract, and then a rather long prayer of grace was said in Afrikaans. Then we all ate.

Later, I sat with Amos and Martha at their table. We talked about their church and soup kitchen, about the apartheid years, about their family and about their work. Amos had given up his job as a motor mechanic to concentrate on his ministry. He told me that for three weeks every year, 'I disappear into the rural district just to rest and read my Bible.' Martha said that she had been a cleaner for 27 years to the same family, but told me that she has never felt appreciated or respected by them. On the other hand, she would never leave them because she promised the dying husband that she would care for his wife. By the end of each working day, during the course of which she earned less than five pounds, Martha fell asleep in a chair. This did not surprise me. On the day when we had this conversation she had been up since five in the morning doing an enormous amount of washing. Amos was quiet as she explained all this. Later he told me that he longed for her to give up what he thinks of as slave labour. Martha, however, had made her promise.

Earlier, Amos had shown me around the neighbourhood. Pointing out the foul-smelling sewage works he said, 'Look what *they* put near our homes.' We talked a bit about the apartheid era and he made this comment: 'They looked for me down there (pointing at the floor) but I was not down there.' And then, holding his hand at eye level he said, 'I was up here.' That's passionate humility. Another comment that he made was about how to speak to people if you seek to influence them. In contrast to the shouting of many preachers, he suggested that one should 'Speak in a low spirit. It sinks in very deeply.'

'Speak in a low spirit.' It would not have been fair for me to ask Amos to explain the phrase more fully. For one thing, I think he was all the while speaking with me in a 'low spirit'. That is calmly, deliberately and seriously but in the context of warm hospitality. It could have been translated as 'Speak with some humility'. Speak to people directly and on the level. Do not tell them what they could or should think or feel or do. To speak with a low spirit, as I understand it, will often involve sharing rather than instructing but it is not primarily a matter of content, for the same content can be expressed in different ways, with different overtones or colours. It is more a matter of *voice*. Voice is where meaning meets integrity, where abstraction is given personality. Voice is where thought meets reality, where word meets flesh. Is it possible, I wonder, to have a Christlike voice?

Jesus before Pilate

One biblical passage that reveals some aspects of the kind of childlike maturity or passionate humility that I am trying to explain here is the encounter between Jesus and Pilate as described by John (John 18.33–38a). The tension of the dialogue and the difference in perspective between the young rural rabbi and the head of the occupying forces comes over most strongly if it is set out as a scene in a play.

Pilate returns to the headquarters. He has failed to convince the leading Jews to deal with the rabbi themselves because they are insisting on the death penalty. Jesus is summoned and stands helplessly before him.

Pilate: Are you the King of the Jews?

Jesus: Do you ask this on your own, or did others tell you about me?

Pilate: I am not a Jew, am I? Your own nation and the chief priests have handed you over to me. What have you done?

Jesus: My kingdom is not from this world. If my kingdom were from this world, my followers would be fighting to keep me from being handed over to the Jews. But as it is, my kingdom is not from here.

Pilate: So you are a king?

Jesus: You say that I am a king. For this I was born, and for this I came into the world, to testify to the truth. Everyone who belongs to the truth listens to my voice.

Pilate: What is truth?

Pilate goes outside to address the Jews again.

At Durham Cathedral we host a breakfast and Bible study opportunity for young adults called '10:05' in which we look at the Gospel reading for the day. When this was the set passage we approached it through drama. Rather than discuss our impressions and interpretations, participants acted it out in small groups. It was remarkable how the character of Pilate changed in the different interpretations. Some were smooth and cynical, others rough and harsh. The contrast with the character of Jesus was quite profound. He came across with great consistency. There was a simplicity and integrity about who he was and what he was saying. While on trial he was not thrown by Pilate's public interrogation. On the contrary, he used the opportunity to identify his priorities and testify to the truth. Our experience was that the *voice* of Jesus comes through this passage no matter who is reading the words.

Earlier in John's Gospel, Jesus speaks of the Good Shepherd and his relationship with his sheep as being encapsulated in the fact that the sheep know the shepherd's voice (John 10.3–5). One of the most astonishing things about Jesus' conversation with Pilate is the way Jesus uses the word 'voice' when we might have expected the word 'words'. Jesus does not say 'Everyone who belongs to the truth listens to my *words*' in verse 37. He says that those who belong to the truth listen to my *voice*. Pilate certainly does not understand what Jesus is talking about here. He entirely fails to pick up on the idea of listening to the voice rather than the words; the thought of attending to the whole rather than the part, the spirit rather than the letter. Indeed, the remark causes him to come out with what is, for modern and western ears, probably the most telling and famous question in the Bible: 'What is truth?' It is a question whose utterance by Pilate establishes beyond doubt that Jesus and Pilate are on completely different wavelengths; that they are talking past each other. Pilate's question reveals that he had not heard the voice of Jesus. For that voice is the question's most profound answer, whether or not it utters the two words, 'I am.'

But Jesus does not reply to Pilate's question. And there is nothing in John's Gospel to tell us how he reacted. But he must have done something. I wish John had told us. Did he begin to give an answer but then give up when he realized that Pilate was not listening? Did he stoop down to write in the dust, as he did on another occasion? Or did Jesus simply stare at Pilate with wide-eyed disbelief and think to himself, 'You really don't get it, do you?'

The Sound of Passionate Humility

Let's get back to Cape Town and the excellent company of Amos and Martha. One evening, they took me to a service in their little shanty church. It was an extremely energetic gathering. A local man called Mr More led the music on his guitar. Amos told me that he was once declared dead but then recovered, to the great surprise and delight of those around him. Amos also valued him because he was able to see 'Tokolsh'. This puzzled me. My puzzlement in turn bewildered Amos. 'They are little people sent by Sangomas to cause trouble.' The explanation was offered with an implicit 'of course' so I did not raise any further question. In the opening song everyone greeted everyone else with handshakes and smiles and kind words. After that I was introduced and prayed for: 'We thank you Lord, for sending the reverend to us – all the way from . . . all the way from . . . all the way from . . . where he has come from.' It was a delightful moment. Really, where I came from was irrelevant. What mattered was that I was 'here'.

People sang in the shanty chapel without any hint of restraint. To say it was uninhibited is accurate but misleading. There was no trace of inhibition. What I heard was absolutely full-on. It was the sound of passionate humility. While some was very good, some was really wild, with several people singing phrases that bore very little relation to the tune being led by Mr More and his guitar. There were specific prayer requests, and certain individuals were asked to turn these into prayer. When individuals prayed (in Afrikaans mostly) so others added words or groans of support. An important request came from a woman whose son was in jail, but was shortly to be relocated from Cape Town to Pretoria. How could he possibly get any family visitors? Towards the end of the service there was a time of 'mass prayer' in which everyone prayed aloud for whatever causes were on his or her heart. It was very noisy and very moving. The songs were simple and there were no books. One consisted of these words repeated over and over: 'Because He loves me, I can face tomorrow.'

I was there to preach and, after my address, people were given the opportunity to ask questions. A very distressed young woman started to speak in excited, staccato, rapid Afrikaans. No sooner had she started, than members of the congregation began to gesture that she was mad and that I should not worry about what she was saying. In fact, the other members of the congregation got quite agitated, raised their voices, and indicated that she should stop talking. Some were trying to shout her down. After she finished, people calmed and there was a silence. Amos then quietly, calmly and deliberately translated what she had said. She had told us that she was living a life of great difficulty with a drunk and abusive husband, often sleeping outside for her own safety. There was no specific question in this, just a need to be heard. Later, I asked Amos what he made of the congregation's attempt to silence her. 'No,' he said, 'we must listen to her.' I then asked him how he would respond if a drunken person came into the church. 'He can stay. We must be kind to him, but he must not misbehave in church. He may wake up in the morning and wonder, "Where was I last night, who were those people who cared for me?"'

The experience of worshipping with this little community in the shanty church was very powerful. If it had not been so worshipful it would have been raucous. I had never experienced such unrestricted singing before. The only time I have heard similar sounds since has been when I have officiated at a wedding for the community of people who own rides and sideshows of travelling fairs, 'show people'. On the whole they don't sing. The men certainly don't, as a matter of pride and identity. However, when the final hymn is 'All things bright and beautiful', things begin to change. It is not that people angelically sing the words but, as the chorus comes round, there is a deep intake of breath and the word 'All' is roared out in a deafening crescendo which puts a smile on everyone's face – if not in the first chorus then certainly by the fourth or fifth. Childlike? Yes. Childish? Probably. But absolutely real.

I sometimes wonder whether these were the sorts of sounds that would have been heard in English parish churches before the days of the pipe organ. The church choir where I was rector once got hold of some music written in the eighteenth century for village churches of the area. It was unsophisticated and unfamiliar and that made it difficult and stilted for us to sing. As we practised it, however, we realized that this music was inviting us to sing in a different, more open, relaxed, full-throated, even bellowing sort of way. The voice required was not a 'choral evensong' or 'Anglican chant' kind of voice, but something more like the sound of football terraces of 50 years ago. To encourage the choir to get into this, I suggested that they should try to 'discover the peasant within'. They laughed and got on with it, and though some found it easier than others, the sound did become a bit earthier and the music started to work. We were really getting into it when the organist, fearing an irreversible change in the sound of the choir, hurriedly put all the copies away.

On reflection, I suppose I was offering an invitation to humility. For this sort of singing comes from somewhere deeper in a person than the level of mere pride or performance. It is more authentic, real and basic than that. And this is exactly how the singing in the shanty church seemed to me. Certainly there were no airs and graces being put on. It was a simple, heartfelt expression of praise and petition to God. I am not being romantic here or idealizing the people of that church. They were not sin-free. The attempt to alienate and silence the distressed woman was also part of the truth of that congregation. But such childish behaviour hardly singles that congregation out. It happens in all churches. Childlikeness and childishness are for ever intermingled in human beings and human communities, including Christian ones. The deeper, more lasting and significant truth of the congregation in the shanty church was that of the manifest *childlikeness*. The unaffected, direct, heartfelt voicing of praise and prayer that spoke of simplicity and trust, joy and humility, was holy in an utterly down-to-earth way. Nothing could have been less disappointing. Nothing could be more childlike and mature; nothing more passionately humble.

Notes

1. Francis, *Adults as Children*.
2. Schopenhauer, *The Pessimist's Handbook*, p. 130.

CHAPTER 6

Giving Up Grumbling

Sitting in the congregation at a cathedral service one Ash Wednesday evening, I felt a bit uncomfortable. I am usually at the front, doing something, so this was not my comfort zone. But that was not the issue. My main worry was that I was not yet sure what my Lenten discipline would be. As I went up for the ashes I felt particularly bad. It was as if I was getting a ticket before deciding whether to catch the bus. As I knelt during the service an idea crystallized. 'How about grumbling', I thought. 'Why not try to avoid grumbling, complaining and finding fault for 40 days and 40 nights?' I was struck by what I felt was the novelty and audacity of the idea. There and then I decided that this would be my Lenten cross. I would not, come what may, grumble or complain.

Once you start to reflect on 'grumbling', you realize that it is a very vague idea, a fuzzy concept. It is sometimes a complaint just wanting to be heard, sometimes a protest seeking to make a difference. Sometimes it is whispered. Sometimes it is shouted. Sometimes grumbles are new and carry a tinge of fresh hurt. Often they have a sad and familiar feel to them. Grumbling is an expression of misery and cynicism. Yet it is a common enough pastime. As someone once said to me about a group of people, 'They are never happy unless they have something to grumble about.' Sadly, however, this cute paradox does not work.

Grumbling undermines happiness, both that of the grumbler and that of his or her audience. It occurs to me that just as beauty is said to be in the eye of the beholder, so grumbling must often be in the ear of the listener. Few of us recognize when we are grumbling or complaining. Rather, we think that we have a good point or that we have a duty to complain. 'I should not have to put up with this.' Grumbling and complaining have become such a habit in us that we do not always spot ourselves doing it. That's the challenge: to spot it coming and take evasive action.

I did not have to wait long after Ash Wednesday for my first test. Two days, in fact. I had been invited to a college to preach. I decided to make a weekend of it, going down on the Friday evening. I had told the college chaplain and he said, 'No problem, I will book you into a college room for three nights instead of one.' However, when I arrived at the Porters' Lodge late in the evening, things did not go quite as easily as I'd hoped. I was booked in for Sunday night, but *only* for Sunday night. By this time all the guest rooms were full. My plan had been to drop my bags in the rooms and then go for a late meal with friends at an Indian restaurant. However, at the time when I was expecting the lager and popadums to appear, I was dragging my bags around the college looking at various desultory and neglected rooms to see whether I might be able to camp in one of them until Sunday. The college porters clearly found this very embarrassing and were profuse and repeated in their apologies. I smiled benignly through this but after a while I realized that my response was arousing their curiosity. College porters are, I suspect, only too accustomed to receiving complaints and hearing grumbles when things don't work out as planned. So I felt I had to explain. 'I might have had a little more to say about this,' I volunteered, 'but I have given up grumbling and complaining for Lent.' They saw the funny side. Immediately the evening was altogether happier.

A few months prior to the grumble-free Lent, I had been able to visit India. While there I had been struck by the absence of complaint and the presence of acceptance. There is a downside to this, of course, and there are levels of corruption, degrees of neglect of corporate responsibility and sheer injustice that should be challenged and overcome. It is certainly possible to be *too* accepting. If no one complains in the face of injustice then injustice simply continues. Part of the shame of India is the way in which the caste system has dehumanized people. One challenging way to begin to understand this more deeply is to read Omprakash Valmiki's autobiography, *Joothan: A Dalit's Life*.[1] The Hindi word 'Joothan' literally means, 'food left on an eater's plate, but which is eaten by someone else'. For a language to have such a word speaks volumes. To have people consigned to living in this way while working as servants is unspeakable. In the book, Valmiki explains how, when he was growing up, he would often have to rely for nourishment on water in which rice had been boiled. Such an existence leaves no time, energy or motivation for grumbling.

Part of the power of the story *Joothan* is that, as time goes by, the author discovered ways of not accepting the injustice which he had inherited. But while protest and anger, rage and resistance were all aspects of his non-acceptance, mere grumbling, tiresome whingeing and habitual complaining had no part at all. It is always so. The mature and effective response to injustice is not complaint but activism; not grumbling about how bad something is but clarifying that it is unacceptable. It is never good enough merely saying that something is wrong. The task is to do something about it. The problem with grumbling is that its dispiriting effect militates against the chances of taking positive action precisely where positive action is needed. In the face of injustice, grumbling is a way to remain part of the problem rather than the solution.

I found the absence of grumbling in India very heartening. In the comfortable and affluent west, grumbling is endemic, complaint is customary and sometimes it even seems compulsory. There is a constant background noise of judgement and assessment regarding everything we do. I have come to the view that this is often less about accountability and improvement and more about vindicating our strange desire to have a good old moan. As an adult educator and trainer, I have, for instance, mostly given up providing people with 'evaluation forms' after training events. I cannot see the point of questions such as 'Rate the venue', or 'Give the speaker marks out of ten'. There is a place for feedback because it helps us to adapt, change, grow and develop. Indeed, it is impossible to imagine learning without feedback. But there are so many ways of giving and receiving it. So I will sometimes offer participants in an event an 'appreciation form' with a few questions, simple and open: 'How was this good and how might we improve it another time?' That's all you need to ask. If it was seriously bad then it is all too evident, and if it was provocatively bad then let people phone up, email or put pen to paper. It can also help to ask people to identify what they have learnt, what they will 'take away' or what they will do differently as a result of attending. Such questions allow people to engage humbly, realistically and responsibly with their own experience without stimulating the critic in them or encouraging them in consumerist arrogance. Indeed, I would go so far as to argue that the mere heading 'evaluation form' can encourage what you might call anti-learning attitudes. It encourages those of us who fill them in to think that what matters is how others could improve their performance, not how I could improve my participation. In a slightly grumpy mood myself, I once imposed a rule for a discussion which said that before you said anything negative you had to say something positive. It was interesting to see how this changed the nature of the debate, how it empowered some and unsettled others. Maybe it is not such a bad idea. We need to earn our entitlement to complain either by genuinely suffering or by offering positive feedback first.

Let me underline the main point. We live in a culture where complaint and grumble have become second nature. I whinge therefore I am. We are habitually, but unnecessarily, critical both with others and with ourselves. A contemporary western education can sometimes encourage this. Our schools and colleges put a premium on developing 'critical faculties'. While this is part of the energy of the humanities, social sciences and sciences, it has the potential downside of leading people to feel chronically disappointed and dissatisfied with their own as well as other people's best efforts. I remember talking with a Cambridge academic about what he called the 'guilt gap'. How it was necessary, if you were to achieve great things, always to be disappointed with yourself. The formula obviously worked for him because he has been highly successful and is now extremely eminent. And complacency is of no use to anyone. There is no virtue at all, never mind humility, in being smug. But there is a little cluster of attitudes which, when taken together, can create a very unhealthy environment, a significantly sick society. I would suggest that the unbridled use of critical faculties, the tendency to find performances disappointing, the sense that one is in some way guilty for not having done better oneself and the easy habit of grumbling about others can all, if unchecked, end up doing more harm than good. Yet for many of us they are everyday activities. They are the bad and damaging habits which consume far too much of our social life. As well as being part of the sickness of our society, they are part of the sickness of our souls. And they are devoid of humility.

Complaining often says more about the speaker than a situation. Going back to India, I recall a hotel room in Pondicherry. In the early hours, I was awake and switched the light on. After a couple of minutes, a rat shot across the floor and sped up the wall to the top of a cupboard. It's the speed of the things that is so alarming. That and the realization this was not the first time a rat had visited the room and that the thin blanket on the bed was, when you looked at it a little more closely, replete with evidence of previous visits. Having shaken all that onto the floor, I kept the light on for the rest of the night and, this being before Ash Wednesday and so before the inauguration of my Lenten discipline of 'no grumbling', I ventured to mention the matter in a negative and disapproving way at the reception desk. It took a while to get the word 'rat' translated into Tamil, but to be honest I don't think it was worth the effort. There's a kind of shrug that tells you all you need to know in any culture. It tells you that your grumbling and complaining are a complete waste of time. It tells you that, if you seriously want things to be different, it's going to take much more time and effort than merely making a complaint.

Benedictine Murmuring

When I set out on my Lenten fast of not grumbling, I was not really sure whether it was an authentic project, a pukka pilgrimage. However, I read these words of Basil Hume a week or so into Lent and took them as a blessing.[2] He speaks of using Lent to turn away from three particular sins: pride, unkindness and then . . .

There is a third thing that separates us from God, which you might find surprising – grumbling.

I learnt this from the Rule of St Benedict, which is constantly telling monks that they must not be grumblers. This is very shrewd. There is nothing worse than living with people who grumble; there is nothing more corrosive than grumbling; nothing more unsettling than grumbling.

This is how Benedict puts it in the Rule: 'First and foremost there must be no word or sign of the evil of grumbling, no manifestation of it for any reason at all. However, if anyone is caught grumbling, let him undergo severe discipline.'[3] It sounds very odd to us to think of someone being disciplined at all, never mind severely, for grumbling. During my Lenten fast, I was caught out in several conversations. 'Is that a grumble?' people would ask if the tone of my remarks became a bit negative or self-pitying. Often it was. This was a bit embarrassing, but fortunately for me no one ever decided to discipline me Benedictine style. Durham Cathedral has some of the best preserved medieval monastic buildings in the country. The cloisters and Chapter House are world famous, but tucked away where the visitors do not go is an old monastic prison cell. It is a dark, cramped and chilling place. Anyone who steps inside is delighted to get out again quickly. It sends a shiver down the spine just to think of young monks being locked up there. I can imagine how, on release, the novice master might have said, 'Now you really do have something to grumble about! But don't even think about it.'

We have learnt to accept our own and other people's grumbles as part of daily life. And yet they never do us any good. No one grumbles in a crisis. Maybe that is one of the attractions of dangerous or exciting pursuits. They create a 'moan-free zone'.

Grumbling is a perverse form of leisure activity which kills time, dampens enthusiasm and eradicates delight. It thrives on self-regard when we are comfortable but envious. When he was taken hostage in Beirut and thrown into a makeshift cell, Terry Waite took a personal vow there and then: 'No self-pity'.[4] Naturally, he would have had no audience for his grumbles other than himself and his intuition told him that his self-pity would only serve to make his experience more difficult. He was right. Self-pity always makes life more difficult and less pleasant.

The 'Why' Question

One of the most common responses that we make to receiving personal bad news is to ask the question 'Why?' This is entirely understandable because the bad news, whether the diagnosis of a terminal disease or the experience of an accident or news of a tragedy affecting a loved one, disrupts our daily life and puzzles us. We are confused and uncomfortable and would like to be getting on with the normal routines of life. When we engage with other people whose lives have been disrupted like this, the bereaved, for instance, we can quickly be influenced by the way in which they are 'taking it'. Some put on a brave face and try to shut out their feelings. This can be denial. Others enter into what is sometimes called a healthy grief process, which can follow any significant loss, not only bereavement. But if denial is unhealthy, so too is its opposite: self-pity. It sounds unsympathetic to say so, but there are times when in pastoral visiting I have found the 'Why?' and 'Why me?' questions to be quite distressing, depressing even. It seems so strange that we should live modern lives, enjoying the benefits of twenty-first-century communications, and not expect that at some time or other our own domestic equilibrium will be disturbed by sickness, death or some other form of tragedy. We know that these things happen, but we never expect them to happen to us. This lack of connection is worth pondering. Maybe it is that we know deep down that it is not worth worrying about these things until they actually happen and demand of us a personal response. (We no more plan for the eventuality of extreme misfortune than we do for astonishing good fortune.) Maybe it is because we rely on the belief that, if they do happen, we will be given graceful resources to cope beyond our imaginings. I fear, however, that it might sometimes be based on a lack of empathy for victims of tragedy, violence and disease whom we have encountered in the past. As one cynical journalist put it, 'The only good news is that you don't know the people caught up in the bad news.' The piquancy of that quip is revealed whenever we find that we *do* know one of the victims of a tragedy.

There are several passages in the Bible where grumbling is identified as a bad thing. In the epistle of James, for instance, we read: 'Beloved, do not grumble against one another, so that you may not be judged' (James 5.9). To grumble is very often to judge others, which is precisely what Jesus teaches us *not* to do. The Pharisees and scribes grumbled when Jesus welcomed sinners and ate with them (Luke 5.30). The most famous biblical complaining takes place in the wilderness, after the exodus from Egypt. Liberated into the freedom of a new and adventurous life, the Hebrew people soon become homesick. Weren't there enough graves for us in Egypt? they grumble (Exodus 14.11). It is as if they were saying, 'Does this Moses really know what he is doing; where he is leading us?' Grumbling is the idiom of the nostalgic and backward-looking. It is the characteristic style of those who were not happy when the past was the present but who, in the present, cannot positively anticipate the future. It is the *lingua franca* of the wilderness until the demons of that place are named and subdued. We grumble when we are disappointed and when we are confronted by disappointment and barrenness. But there are better ways to respond to bad news, tragedy and injustice, all of which are more positive and, paradoxically, more closely connected with genuine, passionate humility.

Protest, Penitence and Petition

Grumbling is a most unattractive, but also a strangely revealing, habit. We can learn a lot about ourselves if we learn how to hear what we are saying when we grumble. When we do, we might well find our self-pitying words to be based on a complex mix of feelings and attitudes. Personal discontent often stems from a lack of both humility and hope. But it might sometimes be based on genuine humility and human solidarity. In this section, I want to suggest that while it is wise to minimize, if not eradicate, our grumbling and complaining, it is sometimes necessary and good, humble even, to give voice to the insight or perception behind the grumble in a different way. In particular I want to suggest the possibilities of protest, penitence and petition. These are all powerful and potentially transformative ways to connect with the causes of our complaints. But to engage in any of them we need the power and confidence that comes not from personal discontent but from realizing that things are in a deep sense 'not right'. The desire for justice and mercy, truth and peace, lies behind all three practices that we explore here. They are all ways in which we express our heartfelt desire for God's kingdom. Once again, we find the engine for passionate humility in the gap between the inauguration and the fulfilment of God's kingdom.

There are occasions when it is right to respond to sadness, disappointment or loss with *protest*. To protest is to commit to making a difference. Grumbling, on the other hand, is being content to make a miserable noise and create a negative atmosphere. When we protest we are aiming our remarks at those whom we believe to be responsible. Protest is a focused and directed outpouring of discontent in which the protestor implicitly takes some responsibility for change. Protest is responsible and impassioned complaint. But it is also vulnerable complaint. When we protest, we stand up to be counted. We put ourselves into the deficiencies of the situation. We inhabit injustice. Protest can carry rage and anger, whether it is expressed politically or prayerfully. Protestors become emotional in prayer or interpersonal exchange and when they demonstrate in public they can, depending on the situation, be photographed, arrested or shot at. The same is never true of mere grumblers. Given the same circumstances, one person might grumble about it and the other mount a protest. It is the one who protests who becomes vulnerable. The fact that some protestors come across as defensive or powerful should not distract us from this truth. To protest or agitate for change is to put yourself into some kind of danger.

On the other hand, there are times when circumstances that make us grumble might more helpfully call us to *penitence*. That might sound an odd suggestion, partly because the word 'penitence' has an unhelpfully heavy ring to modern ears. Penitence can be a helpful and positive alternative to grumbling because it provides a way forward when it is not obvious that all responsibility for a situation is located somewhere else. When we grumble we are distancing ourselves from responsibility for the situation or circumstances we find ourselves in. When we are penitent, however, we kneel down to take a share of responsibility and resolve to share in bringing about some kind of transformation.

This might sound very high-minded, but there are times when such a move might be little more than applied humility. As we become alert to the ecological crisis which has been created by the use of fossil fuels in the pursuit of economic development, so we realize that there is no one person who can stand outside the loop of responsibility, any more than there is one person or group who can take full responsibility for either problem or solution. Similarly, when we realize the scale of the inequality of opportunity for children born in different contexts, not only around the globe but within our own nation, we must appreciate that responsibility is diffuse. This diffuseness can make us feel impotent and miserable. When we grumble about it we encourage others to feel the same. If, on the other hand, we respond with penitence we accept that we have a share of responsibility and bring it to expression in prayer. Thus, when prayers of 'General Confession' are said in church services, we are given the opportunity to express our sorrow not so much for the way things are, but for the way in which our own habits and decisions, as well as our lack of initiative and insight, have all made a contribution to the lamentable state of the world. A classic form of this in the English language is found in the Book of Common Prayer:

> Almighty and most merciful Father,
> We have erred and strayed from thy ways like lost sheep.
> We have followed too much the devices and desires of our own hearts.
> We have offended against thy holy laws.
> We have left undone those things which we ought to have done;
> and we have done those things which we ought not to have done;
> and there is no health in us.[5]

Public, or at least shared, penitential prayer is a very positive alternative to grumbling. And it has very different results. Penitential prayer leads forward to absolution, a reminder and assurance of God's forgiveness of us. The danger of absolution is that it can undermine a sense of personal responsibility. However, absolution is rightly seen by liturgical theologians as connected to baptism, and baptism involves a sense of being commissioned to active discipleship. To quote again from the Book of Common Prayer:

Almighty God, the Father of our Lord Jesus Christ,
who desireth not the death of a sinner,
but rather that he should turn from his wickedness
and live . . .
    Wherefore let us beseech him to grant us true repentance and his Holy Spirit, that those things may please him which we do at this present; and that the rest of our life hereafter may be pure and holy . . .[6]

Contemporary prayers of absolution do not talk about being 'pure and holy'. Rather, they use phrases such as 'Restore you in his image' and 'Raise you to new life in Christ our Lord'.[7] More familiar today, however, is the form of absolution at Communion services where the prayer is that God will not only 'Pardon and deliver you from all sin' but also 'Confirm and strengthen you in all goodness' and 'Keep you in life eternal'.[8] When we dwell on what it might mean to be kept in eternal life, we realize that the absolution is inviting us to continue to seek and anticipate the kingdom of God. In other words, the dynamic of confession and absolution teaches us that when our penitence is heard, we gain new confidence and a new hope. We are no longer merely victims of a cruel world. Rather, we are commissioned as agents of transformation who can venture an effort on the basis that we are acting under the judgement of a forgiving God. Penitence, like all heartfelt prayer and true worship, sends us out 'to live and work to God's praise and glory'. In this way it is very different from grumbling or indulging in self-pity. But we need a significant degree of humility to engage in transformational penitence.

A third possible response when faced with circumstances which might cause us to grumble is to offer a prayer of *petition*. That is, to ask God for what we want or need. The first verse of William Williams' great Welsh hymn of the wilderness is a wonderfully worked example:

> Guide me, O thou great Redeemer,
> Pilgrim through this barren land;
> I am weak, but thou art mighty,
> Hold me with thy powerful hand.[9]

It is the second line which matters. Taken out of context, it could be a grumble: 'Pilgrim through this barren land'. But placed in the context of faith and hope forming themselves into petition, it becomes something far more dignified and positive. When sung with many others to a stirring tune (though *Cwm Rhondda* was never in the mind of the composer), and leading to the impassioned last line of the verse: 'Feed me till I want no more', all thought of grumbling disappears. The negative has been transfigured into positive. This is the simplest spiritual response to hearing ourselves beginning to grumble: to find a way of turning it into prayer and allowing ourselves to be led to praise.

Much has been written about petitionary prayer, and many people worry about it. On the one hand it seems childish and on the other it seems unjust. What sort of God would give us our daily bread only if we ask for it? Does God really reserve parking places for prayerful motorists? Indeed, Jesus told us that 'Your Father knows what you need before you ask him' (Matthew 6.8). And yet the same Jesus tells the story about the woman nagging at a judge until he rules in her favour (Luke 18.1–8). One of the most helpful things I have ever read about petitonary prayer is a sermon by the late Herbert McCabe. It is a lively reminder of the way in which passion and humility combine in petition. McCabe's point is that prayer is for us a process whereby our desires and longings are received and reformed:

> In prayer, then, we do not want to change God's mind, to bring him round to our way of thinking and wanting. Rather it is God who wants us to change our minds, to attend to what he has given, to recognize him, to believe in him and love him and be grateful to him that he is our loving Father.[10]

It follows that it is more important that our prayer is honest than that it is well formed. We need to state and restate our desires until, as we hold them insistently before God, they are gradually transformed. 'Genuine prayer means honest prayer, laying before your Father in heaven the actual desires of your heart – never mind how childish they may sound.'[11] If we learn to pray from our desires truthfully, we will, McCabe assures us, find that our prayer is less distracted. 'People on sinking ships do not complain of distractions during their prayer.'[12] The key is to recognize that prayer requires of us not noble ideals, not generating a list of things we *ought* to want, but something more raw than that.

> We all start as children and we all need time to grow up. It is no good pretending that we are already there. If you treat a 5-year-old as an adult she will never be allowed to grow into

a real adult. If you treat yourself as a saint you will never become one; you will never really want to become one.[13]

Petitionary prayer is a safe place to locate our complaints and our grumbles. They will not change God's mind, but as we shower the heavens with our protests and complaints we will discover that the merciful ears of God not only hear but also begin to transform our words.

The original and perhaps ultimate prayer book for Christians and Jews alike is the book of Psalms. Here the desire is raw and crude, there is no watering down of the passion of the petitioner or grief of the lamenter. The poetry of the psalms is not a way of introducing irony or other devices to distance the writer and the reader or listener but a way of hammering the point home. First the point is made and then, to make sure it is understood, it is made again slightly differently. Among the many images that have the capacity to hold the imagination in sustained and repeated prayer, 'the valley of the shadow of death' ranks high. It refers to a valley so deep that the sunshine never penetrates to its depths. It is the ultimate wilderness, unending darkness. To be a good companion to someone on the journey through that valley is one of the most demanding challenges that any human being can face. But as we enter into caring relationships with those who are suffering in ways that are beyond our imagination, our task is not to feed their self-pity. Indeed, if we are to be a solid and durable companion, we will regret any encouragement to self-pity that we ever offer. There is no companionship more difficult for us than that alongside those who focus their attention on their own misfortune and whose utterances are essentially complaints or grumbles. When companionship gets that difficult, all but the most saintly tend to find other ways to spend their time. Complaining is corrosive of relationships as well as of peace of mind. Benedict knew that monastic murmuring would undermine a religious community and so ruled against it. When we begin to reflect on the impact of grumbling, we realize that it not only undermines our communities, institutions and organizations, it also undermines the grumblers themselves. Whereas humility leads us to delight in simple things and helps us bounce back after disappointment, grumbling keeps us in the valley of dark disappointment.

Grumbling might only be a matter of words, but it too has its victims. Unlike protest, penitence and petition, grumbling lacks both passion and humility. There is no Christlikeness, no wisdom and no maturity in grumbling. It is a good thing to give it up.

Notes

1. Valmiki, *Joothan: A Dalit's Life*.
2. Hume, 'A cheerful, joyous love'.
3. Benedict, *Rule*, chapter 34.
4. Waite, *Taken on Trust*, p. 8.
5. *Book of Common Prayer*.
6. *Book of Common Prayer*.
7. Archbishop's Council, *Common Worship*, p. 31.
8. Archbishop's Council, *Common Worship*, p. 170.
9. *The New English Hymnal*, No. 368.
10. McCabe, *God, Christ and Us*, p. 6.
11. McCabe, *God, Christ and Us*, p. 8.
12. McCabe, *God, Christ and Us*, p. 8.
13. McCabe, *God, Christ and Us*, p. 9.

CHAPTER 7

Becoming a Stranger

As we have seen, while learning humility is integral to discipleship, humility is also integral to learning. Where, then, can we start? In order to break into this circle we need sometimes to allow ourselves to be challenged fairly sharply. Personally I have found the exposure to people of cultural backgrounds different from my own to be a good way of kick-starting a process of renewed adult learning. However, in order to allow the learning to be deep and sustained enough to be formational, rather than merely informative, we often need to augment it with some reflective discipline. Sustained and perhaps facilitated conversation with others going through similar experiences is often profoundly helpful. For me, however, prolonged exposure to cultural difference, conversation with strangers and then the attempt to write about, has often felt like a powerful combination. In this chapter we will reflect quite deeply on the process of adult learning as stimulated by exposure to difference. There are several aspects to this but there is also an underlying narrative of increasing openness to others. This, I believe, is a relational, spiritual and formational process through which we discover that we have more in common with strangers than we thought and that we ourselves are stranger than we had ever dared to imagine. I write here from my own experience not because it is of any intrinsic importance but because the task is to get a sense of the subjective side of the kind of learning that might help form us as people of humility.

Back Home

The first Sunday back in my English parish church after a ten-week visit to South Africa was a disorientating and strange occasion – and not only for the congregation. The previous Sunday I had been taking a service in Soweto while the parish priest was in hospital with tuberculosis. Half of my sermon was translated into Sesotho, half into Zulu. At the end of the service, I blessed all the children by sprinkling each one with holy water. The tradition goes back to the 1970s when no one knew which of the children and young people might not be there the next Sunday, such was the level of violence and fear. The unaccompanied singing was energizing and the people were all keen to participate. Back in England, where the front pews remained resolutely empty and the organ gave an alibi to those a bit too weary or self-conscious actually to sing, the adrenaline did not flow in quite the same way. Having in a few weeks become very comfortable with South African enthusiasm, Church of England reticence felt strange. I felt strange too. After the service someone said, 'I hope you enjoyed your, er . . . I know it was not a holiday.' Fair comment. What had I been up to, away from my duties for over two months? Many people referred to my 'trip' but that felt too slight. The phrase 'study leave' never seemed to catch on. While away I too suffered from some of this confusion and was diffident about how to describe the period of time I was enjoying, spending, using and passing. I tended to alternate between 'study leave' and 'sabbatical', depending on the company. In retrospect, however, it is clear to me that, whatever the fancy words, I had been on a *visit*.

By the word 'visit' I mean to imply something more challenging and changing than a trip. When on a trip we are in observer mode. When we are visiting we engage as people who have opened our hearts and minds to new experience and challenge. Travelling in order to visit creates the possibility of a kind of engagement that is possible while away from the familiar, while out of your 'comfort zone'. Travel does not necessarily broaden the mind. As a radio journalist once commented, 'You can send a turnip around the world but it comes back a turnip.' What you cannot do, in the way I am using the word, is to send a turnip on a *visit*. For built into the idea of 'visit' is openness to experience and to the personal learning and change that may follow.

The South Africa Tourist Board was then advertising with the slogan, 'The world in one country'. It is, of course, an exaggeration, even considering the remarkable diversity of landscape, flora and fauna as well as human culture, but it resonates well with the way that globally significant issues of justice, democracy and human rights, as much as faith and spirituality, have been played out on the South African canvas. The landmark events in recent South African history – the Sharpeville massacre, the imprisonment of Nelson Mandela, the Soweto uprisings, the release of Mandela and the first elections followed by the horrifying and yet hope-filled drama of the Truth and Reconciliation Commission (TRC) – punctuated the second half of the twentieth century. The struggle in South Africa has been symbolic of the unfolding drama along the fault-line of the relationship between the 'haves' and the 'have-nots' as it has developed in the last half-century. This relationship, this struggle for justice, has been configured as that between rich and poor or oppressor and oppressed, but in South Africa has been drawn in explicit and concrete terms as that between black and white and, more recently, between victim and perpetrator.

South Africa is also a place with a strong Anglican Church and where English is widely used. These last two points gave me a proximity to the everyday life of people in different kinds of community and access to some of the deeper issues at stake in society as well. At the time it was not entirely clear to me how extraordinary the variety of the social, economic and religious encounter and hospitality that I experienced was. The penny finally dropped in a café in Johannesburg where I struck up a conversation with a young couple from Cape Town who had come to the 'city of gold' to get ahead in life. I was casually relating some of the places I had been staying when their faces took on a rather glazed expression that caused me to dry up in mid-sentence. After a brief pause, one of them said, 'That's so amazing. We white South Africans could never go to all those places and be involved in all those things. It simply would not happen.' I knew that I had enjoyed the last couple of months, that some of my excursions had been difficult to organize and that some eyebrows were raised when I proposed certain visits. But it was at this moment that the extent to which I had been not only crossing but transgressing boundaries began fully to dawn on me.

Something Understood

Writing was a crucial aspect of the transformative personal effect of my visits in South Africa. While there, I wrote a journal in which I recorded where I went and what I did. I summarized key conversations and recorded some of the thinking that I was able to engage in and my efforts to try to put some of my experiences into words. Writing the journal was integral to the process of absorbing and understanding those experiences, but I soon discovered that the profound, the surprising, the truly meaningful do not fall into words very easily. One response to this is to reach for words that don't describe anything so much as communicate our bewilderment. There are some times, some experiences, some reflections or conclusions that just do not seem to fit into the language and the structures of thought that serve us reasonably well most of the time. We feel that there is something inexplicable, maybe even completely ineffable, about these experiences, and so we adopt a more spiritual, supernatural or theological language. Walter Brueggemann has drawn attention to the extent to which the sensation of 'amazement' and the word 'astonished' are used in the Gospels.[1] We are astonished when something happens that we cannot describe in the same way as the rest of our experience or with our established everyday vocabulary. It is at this point of surprise and strangeness that we reach beyond the range of our normal vocabulary and find words like 'miracle' or 'grace'. I noticed this when speaking with some Jews and Hindus about what they made of the TRC and the transition to democracy. As one person said, 'Here I must use a word I do not usually utter, indeed I think of it as a Christian word . . . Basically it was a *miracle.*' His hesitancy and yet confidence in using this strange word has caused me to reflect on what was going on here. People only reach beyond their normal lexicon under certain circumstances. They use strange words to mark the strangeness of experience. We do this when we are surprised in a deep way. Equally, when we encounter a person or a community that has qualities and characteristics that we perceive but cannot label, we feel inarticulate, surprised, astonished. On these occasions, I believe that we must put on hold the young Wittgenstein's instruction that 'Whereof we cannot speak we must remain silent' and recognize that this is an opportunity to engage in the spiritual and intellectual struggle of trying to put the surprising and the astonishing into words.

As I prepared for my visit to South Africa, I was aware that I was generating some rough hypotheses, and framing certain kinds of propositions, especially regarding reconciliation, which was the focus of my interest. In the early part of my stay, I felt that I was collecting observations and experiences and then sifting and organizing them in terms of the categories that had been prepared through my reading. It was not long, however, before I realized that much of what was going on within and around me did not fit into my ready-made categories. I accepted this with some equilibrium, feeling that I needed to have a few new categories and maybe learn a few new concepts or ideas, in order to make sense of what I was experiencing and what I was hearing from others. This process continued for a while. But it was much later in my stay, indeed it was while reading a pamphlet, sitting in a car park in Durban, waiting for someone to get his cell-phone fixed, that something clicked. It was at this point that I first appreciated that what was going on was far more than the informal collecting of data or even the creating of new categories to make sense of my discrete observations. No, I felt that what was going on was more like an intellectual and spiritual 'paradigm shift'. To use other jargon, one could say that this was an experience of *metanoia*, a realization that my mind as it was, my 'old mind', was not actually capable either of adequately making sense of the reality I had experienced or wisely guiding my decisions. Quite what the new mind would be like, I could not yet say. It was going to take time to emerge. But I felt even clearer that something like this was going on when I returned to my parish where all the people greeted me as if I was returning relatively unchanged. It was the welcome that made me feel strange. 'Hello stranger,' they said. 'Stranger than you think,' I thought. But I was different not because I had absorbed lots of new impressions and experiences, but because I had changed, adjusted to them at a level deeper than ordinary thought or speech.

The process of writing while visiting was integrally related to this change of mind, this deep learning and adjustment. The visit was, in essence, a time of being open to significant experience and new reality. My journal was therefore the exercise of narrating an experiment with openness. The visit and the journal were part of the same process in that the writing was intended not to bring experience to a closure but to open it up still further. This is exactly what happened as I tried to record what I was seeing, hearing and feeling. I was attempting to use my vocabulary and grammar to do justice to things that not so much informed as *astonished* me. After a while I realized that my attempts to understand were doomed. But I was also aware that, unless we really try hard to understand, we will not sufficiently challenge our existing, inadequate categories of thought and break through to something more adequate. More than that, we will miss the opportunity to transcend thought itself and get lost in wonder and contemplation.

As adults we are often tempted to assimilate or absorb our experience in the terms and categories that have stood us in good stead in the past. But if we are to learn in a deeper and more meaningful sense, what is required of us is something altogether more challenging. We must recognize and accept the mental pain that is a crucial part of the internal adjustment that I have been describing before we can engage with the new, the different, the other, on its own terms. The natural tendency is to become defensive when we feel it arriving. But as people of passionate humility, Barefoot Disciples, we must learn how to welcome this mental pain. The alternative is to resist the learning process and remain stuck in a limited and limiting understanding of ourselves, the world and God.

John Hull writes passionately about the many ways in which Christian adults do *not* learn. Given what we have said about learning as an intrinsic and fundamental component of discipleship, this is deeply ironic. In terms of Christian vitality it is tragic. Hull describes the way in which the reluctance or inability of Christian adults to engage in learning contributes to the formation of particularly dull Christian character. He sees two underlying causes of this: one is the 'need to be right' and the other the inability to accept the 'pain of learning'.[2] He argues that typical experiences of Christian worship serve to encourage people in this non-learning sort of Christianity. They encourage 'dreamy rumination' rather than actual engagement with what people really believe and care about. Hull believes that it is actual engagement with others which opens up the learning process. He stresses that young people are an important part of the mix here. That fits with what we have said about childlike maturity. Unless we are able to ask questions and entertain possibilities in a childlike way, we are unlikely to learn anything new. My own experience suggests that it is encounters with the childlike, rather than with those who are young, that makes the difference. Childlike strangers, those with both maturity and openness, are perhaps the most transformational company we can expect to keep. Certainly such encounters can be highly energizing; they have the capacity not only to humble us – a fair response to hearing the stories of many of our sisters and brothers across the planet – but also to engage our passion, our energetic concern that they might become inheritors and inhabitants of the kingdom of God.

Concluding his reflections on the resistance of many adult Christians to the pain of learning, Hull offers a scary caricature of the adult Christian who is locked in a cycle of non-learning. He describes them as 'jaded, timid, vague, polite and sometimes eccentric personalities'.[3] This is what you become, he believes, if you are formed by dull expressions of Christian worship and life. Personally I don't find anything wrong in eccentricity or politeness. 'Jaded, timid and vague' are, however, a long way from the emerging picture of a Barefoot Disciple which has been developing in these pages. They are not the qualities of people of passionate humility.

Openness and Empathy

A key question for us is what to do about our ignorance. Sometimes we cover it up by saying 'I don't know' in a way which implies, 'And why should I? As far as I am concerned, anything which bewilders me does not actually make sense at all.' All too rarely do we say, 'I simply do not understand, but I wish that I could adjust the way I think so that at last all this would make some sort of sense to me.' Yet the desire to understand that which is currently mysterious, while accepting that at the end of the day much of it will remain mysterious, is a quality which is deeply connected with humility. We might want to call this desire for wisdom, 'openness'.

Openness is about the way in which we observe and the way in which we allow our attention to be directed and guided. We have to learn how to notice, to hear and to see. This is difficult because in order to survive and flourish we need to filter out much, if not most, of what is going on around us. This is increasingly apparent in the 'information age' where we are bombarded by messages all the time. But there is nothing new about it. It is part of the human condition. As a famous quotation from George Eliot's *Middlemarch* puts it:

If we had a keen vision and feeling of all ordinary human life, it would be like hearing the grass grow and the squirrel's heart beat, and we should die of that roar which lies on the other side of silence. As it is, the quickest of us walk about well wadded with stupidity.[4]

To be open, we need to have reached some kind of mastery over the subconscious perceptual filters which constantly limit our experience and render the world less frightening, but also less interesting, challenging and vivid than it really is. Left to themselves, these filters, George Eliot's 'wadding', will eliminate from our perception all the evidence that we need to adjust and to learn. Sigmund Freud called this wadding 'defence mechanisms' and argued that they are necessary for psychological survival. When they are operating well, they moderate the threats and shocks that impinge on us from the real world. It is as if our psyche adjusts its doors and windows so as to keep reality at bay. Ideally, this screening will keep out bad and distressing information. But sadly, we sometimes screen out too much and so fail to appreciate realities that are of decisive significance for us as human beings. In Eliot's terms, our wadding is too thick. When it is, we will not only fail to pick up on bad news but we will also fail to develop qualities like empathy.

The moral and spiritual importance of empathy came home to me one day in the chapel of Durham Prison. I was there with a small group of clergy during Prisons Week. We shared the opening session with a few prisoners who, had we not been there, would have been using the space for their regular faith group meeting. The most confident member of the group told us something of his story. He focused on the way in which his participation in the group had led to baptism and how this whole process was changing him as a person. It was a stumbling, heartfelt and moving presentation, full of humility and honesty. Talking with him afterwards, I learnt more about his life and his crime. I also learnt more about his journey of personal development and faith. What really surprised me was that his main discovery seemed to have been the fact that his actions had caused pain and hurt to others. Until quite recently that had been a complete blind spot for him. As time was going by, however, he was becoming more alert to the feelings and needs of others, more sensitive to their pain or distress. In a word, he was learning empathy.

I was a little taken aback by this. I am not sure that I had previously thought of empathy as something we need to learn. I felt it just happened. Now I think of it, this seems absurd. As children we have very little sense of the trouble we cause, we just expect our needs to be met and protest loudly if they are not. It is only by growing into something like maturity that we begin to develop a sense of how others are feeling, thinking, reacting and responding to our presence and our actions. These days we call these qualities 'emotional intelligence'. That little phrase should not make us think that they are an unlearned or unearned endowment. Like other aspects of character, they are learnt through the rough and ready processes of formation that we call everyday life.

Encountering the prisoner who was beginning to learn empathy alerted me to my failure to appreciate that empathy is something that needs to be learnt. Might it be, however, that my failure is much the same as his? It is a failure of empathy not to appreciate that others have little or no empathy. This means that, ultimately, the prisoner and I are in the same boat. And we will be joined by anyone who realizes that there are limits of which we are not aware to our sensitivity and compassion, sympathy and empathy. It is common for people who visit those in prison to say, 'There but for the grace of God go I.' Another way of putting it might be: 'There but for the grace of empathy, go I.'

Or, maybe we should go one step further and learn how to say, 'There by the grace of empathy, *I am.*' That, it seems to me, is where the pathway of passionate humility will take us: to a place of shocking and sobering solidarity.

The power of the new, the shocking and the astonishing is that it somehow gets past our defences and starts to trouble us. It can come through reading, conversation or art, or through profoundly new experiences or events which not only shock but also rock and undermine us. It is intentionally brought about when young offenders are brought face to face with their victims, as sometimes happens in restorative justice programmes. A good counsellor or spiritual director might create a safe space where we can knowingly let our defences down. For those who can tolerate more risk, the adventure of new or different experiences can crash through them like a tsunami. A key skill of adult educators is to encourage people to be open to whatever it is that will set them thinking for long enough to elicit a deep emotional response which shows that some real change is happening within. Such deep learning is facilitated in many ways, but a shock to the system, or a surprising stimulus to the imagination, can sometimes kick-start it. When it does, we can allow the process to grow and develop by attempting to describe new reality in terms of the old structures of thought. This is the difficult project of writing, for which the best possible image is a piece of paper being screwed into a ball and thrown across the room. This happens when we know that something is wrong with what we have written. That something about it does not capture the reality that is impinging upon our minds and crying out to be both understood and communicated. It happens when we are clear that the sense on the page is not the same as the sense in the world; when we apprehend that the eyes managed to see something, or the ears hear something, that cannot be processed into an account by our existing intellectual apparatus. It is at this moment that we realize that note-taking has come to an end and that we cannot merely *record* the experience. It is the time, the moment, the *opportunity* for deep and transformative thought. The churning of the categories must begin. What we might call personal formation, or even reformation, must proceed.

The Strangeness of Myself

Maybe, then, we really can distinguish between a *trip* and a *visit*. Genuine visiting can be undermined by the habits that we have acquired to help us make diverting trips. Taking photos, buying souvenirs, thinking through events in such a way as to turn them into amusing anecdotes for the dinner table (or even illustrations to be used from the pulpit) can all get in the way of the openness that underlies true formation. Ironically, it is precisely when one goes into observer-mode that openness is lost. Precisely in order to observe, we put our empathy and our connectedness on hold. Merely to observe is implicitly to evaluate, to treat the object that we are observing precisely as that: an object, what Martin Buber famously called an 'it'. If we are ourselves to become learners in a deep sense we will need to open ourselves, to put to one side the desire for objectivity. On the prison visit when I met the man who was learning empathy, the chaplain encouraged us all to pay some attention to our feelings during the experience. They were not always comfortable. But as we have seen, the path to relationships and learning necessarily involves self-awareness and the capacity to reflect on our own feelings. Only if we are prepared to do this are we able to enter meaningfully and helpfully into the experience and reality of others. In other words, when we are challenged to relate to people we not only do not know but find bewildering and strange, we are simultaneously challenged to understand ourselves in a new light – theirs. And that involves seeing the strangeness of our self.

While I was in South Africa I did not read very much. My encounters and experiences gave me more than enough to think about. I knew that I needed time to 'process it all' as we say. The few things that I did read, however, made a very big impact on me, perhaps because of the openness that the visit had engendered. My defence mechanisms had been prised wide open. I thirstily drank in anything that I read. Like Amos' words spoken in a low spirit, they went in very deep. One day I was able to spend some time in the reading room of the Centre for the Study of Violence and Reconciliation in Johannesburg. I came across a recently published book of essays and one caught my eye immediately. Written by Geraldine Smyth, a Dominican nun in Northern Ireland, it argues that part of the point and power of what she calls a 'pilgrim journey' is to cross boundaries and to *become* a stranger.[5] The idea stopped me in my tracks. This is precisely what was happening to me in the course of my travels. My journey, which was both to South Africa and across the boundaries that were so deeply and physically etched into that country and the minds of its peoples by the apartheid years, was not only about discovering the strangeness of others but also the strangeness of myself.

I had come to South Africa to learn about forgiveness and social reconciliation but found myself engaged in personal reconciliation and self-discovery. As I reflected on Smyth's article and my experience of crossing boundaries and barriers in the new South Africa, it became clear that reconciliation is not something that occurs only, or even primarily, 'out there' but significantly 'in here', in the complexity of our minds, the affections of our hearts and the marrow of our bones. Having come to this place to learn about the reconciliation needed after decades of apartheid, I began to realize that reconciliation is not something that is occasionally necessary because things have gone wrong or people have become alienated. Rather, reconciliation is the project that we are always engaged in because our experience is fundamentally of diversity and division, of observing or crossing boundaries and hearing, but also owning, a plurality of voices and identities. As such, it is profoundly based on empathy.

Encountering those whom we don't, and possibly can't, understand can impact on us in different ways. The starkest alternatives are that it might cause us to shrink back in fear or motivate us to open up into dialogue. Either will impact on our conversation partner, but we will only ever learn or grow when we are open enough to stay with the other in dialogue of some kind. Only a sustained, open engagement will allow us to adjust, accommodate and learn in response to realities which were previously beyond our experience. To be mature, in my view, is not to have got to a pinnacle or plateau in this process, but to have learnt how to delight in it. To be wise is not so much to see the sense on the far side of our confusion or the order beyond our current chaos, as to trust ourselves to venture into the confusion and chaos. Openness, or wisdom, demands that we take the risk of being overwhelmed, that we render ourselves vulnerable to the unknown and uncertain. It does so because its vision of God is so utterly transcending and its faith in God's love is invincibly strong. This foolish but wise vulnerability is all of a piece with passionate humility. And we will be closer than ever to this virtue when we take the risk of *visiting* others. For it is in the encounters that we can call visits that we develop openness, become strange, and allow ourselves to be formed in the likeness of Christ.

Hospitality

In this chapter we have explored some of the deep practices of personal learning that happen when we are exposed to new and bewildering realities. This has led us to appreciate that our own self is strange to others. This in turn has suggested that visiting, when accompanied by a spirit of openness, can be a profoundly formative experience. It is humbling in the deepest sense, whether or not we use that phrase to describe it. To balance this deep and personal process I want to suggest that we can engage in a similar learning process much closer to home if we begin to take the practice of hospitality with due seriousness.

In my early years as a parish priest, I was concerned about the quality of welcome that we gave to people coming to church. Having discussed the subject in the Parochial Church Council (PCC) a few times, we formed a committee to consider the matter. There is nothing remarkable about that except that onto it went three people who had been part of the church for a long time and three people who were new to the church. I did not attend their meetings but encouraged the new people on the group to work hard to explain to the old hands their experience and feelings on first coming to the church. Several months later the group reported. The PCC was hushed as the chairman, a churchwarden, unfolded his piece of paper and began to explain the group's findings. They had identified the key problem. There was an excited silence. 'It's the door!' Like many medieval and Victorian churches the door was made of solid oak. This one was exceptionally large and, depending a bit on the weather, could be difficult to open. As people approached it for the first time, he told us, they were anxious about what would appear as they looked, or bravely ventured, inside. Certainly the door was difficult to open, but it was even more difficult to look and then venture inside.

Not only had the committee identified the problem, they also came up with a solution. It was to station someone, we called that person a 'welcomer', outside the door to greet everyone, regulars and strangers alike, and to open the door if it was not already ajar. If the person was new or nervous, the outside welcomer could talk with them a little and introduce them to someone who 'knew the ropes'. This provision was not the end of our work on welcome but it was a very significant beginning. The issue was the door and what happens around it.

'Welcome' sounds like an easy word, but all sorts of issues, agendas and anxieties get muddled up with it. I was once welcomed with these words at a church meeting in a former factory. 'We are so glad you are with us. I bet you are missing your own church. Never mind, this is your church today.' The welcome was five star, though I confess that I felt rather uneasy with much of what followed. In Anglican churches there is often a concern that the welcome should not be too effusive. We tend to aim at a *warmish* welcome to church, but would much rather err on the side of it being too cool than too hot. I have found that whenever the subject is raised, someone soon says that people don't want to be smothered. Then all the introverts fold their arms and nod in silent support.

Hospitality, however, is intrinsic to any attempt to be a Christian community, which, whether we like the idea or not, is what we do when we celebrate the Eucharist together. This is why Benedict was so deliberate about the processes of hospitality in his Rule. It is an emphasis that has stayed with religious communities and which has profound and far-reaching effects. Even today, those who visit monastic houses are often impressed by the quality of welcome they receive. Such welcome is humility in action, the sort of humility which recognizes the stranger as the neighbour. I can certainly remember my first visit to a convent. I must have been about nine years old when I visited, together with my siblings and parents, the convent in Wales where my mother grew up. I was not at all familiar with the ways of nuns or the architecture of convents. I remember exploring the place and finding that my nosiness was rewarded with an amazing olfactory safari. There was the smell of polish in the hall, incense in the chapel, soup in the kitchen and dining room, and carbolic soap everywhere upstairs. It was a fascinating place and I recall it vividly. I also recall the welcome we received. There was a tremendous fuss from one or two of the older nuns when we arrived. This seemed like slightly eccentric but easily recognizable extended family behaviour. These nuns came across to me as particularly odd great-aunts. Then every few minutes, and then every few hours, a new nun would appear, though to my nine-year-old eyes they all looked the same. Each new nun would simply and deeply say how welcome we were. She would speak directly and straightforwardly and make eye-contact with each one of us, children as well as adults, before scuttling off. It was profoundly welcoming and very respectful. It communicated hospitality with realism and warmth. And there was no smothering! Little did I know that behind this direct and sincere greeting was Benedict's dictum about welcoming guests as Christ. Nor did I make any connection between the quality of that welcome and the welcome that my mother would have received when she arrived there when she was just two years old. At that time, she would have been a very insecure and vulnerable person, bewildered by everything she encountered, including the strange words and accents, for she had been in France since her birth. Yet she was welcomed and able to make her home there for twelve years. Clearly her own life would have been very different had that community not been hospitable, kind and loving.

Most, if not all, hospitality, is remarkably mundane. Hospitality is usually about being generous with the domestic and personal stuff for which we are responsible, in particular our time and our space. Nonetheless, I am losing track of the number of transformational moments I am aware of which have taken place in the arena of hospitality. And all who venture into the world of inter-faith dialogue know of occasions when food has been shared, perhaps after a day of shared fasting in Ramadan. I recall visits to my former parish church by adults and children of different faiths in a similarly vague but deeply impressed way. On one occasion a group of twelve turbaned and bearded Sikhs came to visit the church. As they left, we stood outside the ancient building to have a photograph taken. Later, I sent them copies. More than a decade after that, I met one of them again. He told me that he had framed that photograph and put it on the wall of his home in India. 'Everyone who visits my home likes this photo,' he said, 'and they say, "Who is this English gentleman?" Then I tell them of our work of getting different faiths together here in the UK and they find it very inspiring.' There are layers of both hospitality and fun in that story, as there are in so many.

When our children were young, we had a priest from South India to stay with us for a fortnight. He was a stranger, but he came with a good recommendation. At his first meal with us he said, 'You need to know that I don't say "Thank you" because while I am here I feel that you are my family and we don't say "Thank you" in the family. Also, I don't cook or do domestic work.' Some people might have felt uncomfortable with that, but we enjoyed it. Our guest was taking us into his life and experience and culture while at the same time absorbing ours. He did so with many interesting stories that brightened our lives, broadened our horizons and animated our conversation at meals. His name in Tamil means 'light' and he brought light into our home. Having such guests makes a big impact on the whole household.

Children's eyes are opened by those who sit at table with them, and so too are those of adults who have childlike maturity.

The same spirit of openness that we saw as being integral to discipleship learning is integral to hospitality. Hospitality is not just about welcoming people to your home or church or institution, but about letting them into you, letting them past Freud's defence mechanisms and George Eliot's 'stupid wadding'. The Mennonite pastor and writer, Michele Hershberger, invited some friends to take part in what she called the 'Forty Day Experiment'. It was very simple. Each day each participant was to pray, 'Lord, please send me a hospitality opportunity today.' They were then to journal and discuss what happened. One of the fruits of this was a remarkable book in which she shares some of the lessons and reflections that came out of the experiment. One was exactly this sense of the guest/host role reversal:

> In true hospitality, the guest many times becomes the host. The healing that transpires in the act of hospitality happens to the host as well as the guest. The roles blend and merge, gifts are exchanged, and the divine is present.[6]

This aspect of hospitality is powerfully evident in some of the Gospel stories where Jesus is at table with others. For instance, on the road to Emmaus, Jesus is the stranger who becomes guest who becomes host (Luke 24.13–35). In the story of Zacchaeus there is the same dynamic (Luke 19.1–10). In both cases, there is profound transformation and reorientation of life. This point is made poetically in a Eucharistic hymn by George Briggs, my predecessor in Loughborough:

Come risen Lord, and deign to be our guest;
Nay, let us be thy guests; the feast is thine.
Thyself at thine own board make manifest,
In thine own sacrament of bread and wine.[7]

The point is simple but crucial. George Macleod used to use this simple grace at table: 'Christ our Host. Christ our Guest. Amen.' The word 'guest' is significant. When we are away from home we do well to think of ourselves as *visitors* and to behave with due courtesy and respect for our hosts. When we are at home, on the other hand, we should think of those whom we might call visitors as *guests*. This is especially important for institutions which are developing an ethos of Christian hospitality, for it is only when we think of visitors as guests that we will recognize that we are at one with them because we too are guests of Christ. The word 'guest', like the practice of hospitality, is part and parcel of the lived and shared humility of Christian fellowship. Its use is a hallowing and reconciling habit.

Notes

1. Brueggemann, *The Prophetic Imagination*, pp. 96–108.
2. Hull, *What Prevents Christian Adults from Learning?*, pp. 89–143.
3. Hull, *What Prevents Christian Adults from Learning?*, p. 143.
4. Eliot, *Middlemarch*, p. 226.
5. Smyth, 'Brokenness, Forgiveness, Healing and Peace in Northern Ireland', p. 333.
6. Hershberger, *A Christian View of Hospitality*, p. 27.
7. *The New English Hymnal*, No. 279.

CHAPTER 8

Living Generously

Travel is a great way to learn, but you never know what the lesson will be. One day I took a long journey across south India. It started with a train journey and ended up with a bus ride. The train leg was relaxed and fun. My companion and I spent a lot of time talking to some friendly law students. Subjects ranged from corruption to communication via religion. When they discovered that I was a Christian priest, they could not contain their surprise. One of them, a law student who also worked for a TV company, gave me his view of religious people. 'They are like politicians,' he declared, 'far too wordy: I do not like the blah, blah.' It reminded me of a phrase I had heard in England. 'People have had it with words.' There is truth in this insight. When teaching about the generosity of God, Jesus once said, 'Is there anyone among you who, if your child asks for a fish, will give a snake instead of a fish? Or if the child asks for an egg, will give a scorpion?' (Luke 11.11 and 12). The sadness is that, all too often, we disciples of Jesus offer the world not what it wants and needs, which is vision and meaning, compassion and encouragement, but words that do not connect. We dole out the 'blah, blah'. This is not only sad, it is tragic. The words are kindly and sincerely meant, and are offered in a spirit of generosity. The problem is not about our intentions. It is that there is something wrong with our generosity. *Unlike* God, we do not give people what they need. We give them what they do not need: more words. We just love preaching. And we do it in so many ways, from giving advice to issuing statements, from making pronouncements to publishing positions. It is not intended this way but it can easily come across as more and more 'blah'. Christianity is never at its most attractive when it is at its most talkative. Generosity with words is not the same as true generosity. Less is more, just about every time. There is a lot to be said for not saying too much.

After the train we took an auto-rickshaw to the 'bus stand' (station) in a remote town in order to catch the bus for the next leg of our journey. It had been raining very heavily. The puddles were deep and the mud thick. The bus stand was a cross between a market, a farmyard and the regional rubbish tip. As well as the ubiquitous cows and goats, a family of pigs was wandering about. The small sheltered area had a concrete floor, covered with large ants scavenging away around rotting food. We had a long wait for a bus, so went for some tea. Tea involves boiling both water and milk, so we thought it would be pretty safe. But we would not have been persuaded to eat there, even if we were desperate.

It is not easy to get the right bus in rural Tamil Nadu if you cannot read Tamil. So we had to rush from bus to bus asking where it was going and hoping someone would be able to translate for us. We had a large bag which made it even more difficult to make progress across the slippery mud to get to every new bus that arrived and try to work out its destination. Eventually someone wrote a time and some numbers on my companion's hand and gave us a rough idea of which puddle our bus might park next to. We found this bus after our tea and struggled aboard. It smelt like a fishmonger's shop and there was indeed a packet of fish at the back. Towards the front of the bus sat many women from the fishing community. These women have a local reputation for being very fierce and confrontational. Someone said to us, 'Those women and an argument are never separated.' As the bus sped along with the doors and windows open, the conditions did become a little more comfortable. The bus seemed full to me, but when we stopped in the various villages along the way, more people squeezed on and no one got off. When the bus was absolutely crammed full, the rain started again. It was the last blast of the monsoon. Quickly the doors and windows were closed. Immediately you could feel the temperature and humidity rising rapidly – like a fever in a TV cartoon.

The end of the journey was the worst bit. The bus stopped at our next destination and some people jumped off. Others started to get on. Many more wanted to get off, including us, but we also had to pick up our bag which was wedged behind a seat at the front. With people getting both on and off, the bus started to reverse. There was a lot of shouting but all the activity continued. I was not far from the door but did not want to get off without my heavy bag, which was very close, but with so many people between me and it, absolutely unreachable. More people tried to get on – and off. Then there was some very shrill and scary shouting from some of the women. People took notice of that and there was soon some order and calm. The bus stopped. All the women got off, giving me the microsecond of opportunity to grab and extract my heavy bag and jump free, narrowly avoiding a puddle, slipping in the mud but not quite falling over.

It was an unforgettable journey, and I will be happy if the experience is never repeated. I was sure that I was not going to get my hands on that bag again, and that aggravated my stress enormously. I did not realize it at the time, but that was the second lesson of the day. For just as the young law students were clear that religion and politics are focused far too much on words, 'the blah, and blah', so I came to realize that we invest far too much of ourselves, of our souls, in our possessions.

One day a rich young man came to ask Jesus what he must do to inherit eternal life. Jesus told him that he must keep the commandments. After a brief exchange they ascertained that the young man was well up to speed in terms of keeping commandments. But Jesus then changed gear and said to the rich young man, 'If you wish to be perfect, go, sell your possessions and give the money to the poor, and you will have treasure in heaven; then come, follow me' (Matthew 19.21). Unlike many religious teachers who might have gone into discussion with the young man about the detail of what it means to keep the law, Jesus cut through to the issue that was actually inhibiting this person. Jesus saw that for all his righteousness in the law, this man was oppressed and confined by his things. The proof that Jesus was right about this is seen in the man's reaction. 'When the young man heard this word, he went away grieving, for he had many possessions' (Matthew 19.22). It caused the man to *grieve*. That reaction is worth noting. We usually talk about grief when a loved one has died. But the man was grieving the loss not of a person but the prospect of the loss of his possessions.

Possessions are often more significant than we think or let on. Sometimes people distinguish between crimes committed against people and those committed against property. In reality, it is not so simple. Certainly there is a difference between being a victim of Grievous Bodily Harm and having your laptop pinched on the train. When people's homes are burgled, the difference is not so clear. Words like 'violation' can apply to the feeling that people have been in the intimate places of your home helping themselves to the choicest of possessions and making a mess of the rest. In the parables of the lost coin and lost sheep in Luke 15, the losses lead to searches which end only when there can be a party to celebrate what has been found. These stories only work as parables because the experience of losing does so much to awaken us to the true value of things. Our things, our stuff, our possessions, *do* matter to us. They get entwined into our self-understanding. They are markers that help us remember who we are. They are the tokens that help us feel secure in and about ourselves. But, as Jesus saw, they can also get in the way of our discipleship and faith. That is why he told the rich man not only to give away his money but first to sell all his things. They were getting between him and the kingdom of God.

The spirituality of possessions kicks in powerfully when we move house. People sometimes distinguish between hoarders and others. I think it is more accurate to say that with remarkably few exceptions, we are all hoarders, but to varying degrees. On the whole, the longer we live, the more we have hoarded and the more we hoard. This means that leaving the building that has been the family home for decades can be a massively difficult wrench, an elderly identity crisis. Those who must 'downsize' or move into sheltered accommodation inevitably have to face the full weight of the burden of possessions. Then, at the next stage, when the prospect of moving into a residential care home appears, the crisis only gets worse. There are pluses to such a move, of course: good central heating, the lifts, and the access to care. On the downside is the institutional food, and, as I have heard many people complain, the company: 'Why have they put me with all those old people?' But it is the thought of not having 'my own things' that is the deepest wrench.

The Rich

One of the problems we have in relating to Jesus' demand to the rich young man that he undertake the heroic stance of voluntary poverty, is that we do not classify ourselves as being rich. Richard Harries writes that when people heard about his series of lectures addressing the question, 'Is there a gospel for the rich?', they said, 'I must ring my wealthy friends and persuade them to come.'[1] They had already missed the point. Simply to own things is, in a global and historical context, to be rich. Most people do not have very much stuff at all. To own even one book sets you instantly in the privileged minority. Nonetheless, we never quite appreciate that we are rich because our attention is guided by envy to those who are richer than we are. If we could let generosity direct our attention, it would go the other way. For capitalism to work, of course, we must constantly aspire to be wealthier. Ultimately there is no future in this: 'The lover of money will not be satisfied with money; nor the lover of wealth with gain. This also is vanity' (Ecclesiastes 5.10).

Three of the most well-known phrases in the New Testament are directly concerned with what we might call the dark side, the dangerous quality, of money. 'You cannot serve God and wealth' (Matthew 6.24; Luke 16.13); 'The love of money is the root of all kinds of evil' (1 Timothy 6.10); and 'Render to the emperor [Caesar] the things that are the emperor's, and to God the things that are God's' (Matthew 22.21). Of these, it is the third which is the most radical. It comes as the punch-line at the end of a tetchy encounter between Jesus and an unholy alliance of Pharisees and Herodians. Together, they set a trap by facing Jesus with a closed question about paying taxes. From their perspective the only answers were 'Yes' or 'No' and both would get Jesus into hot water. But, as so often, Jesus declined to answer the question as set and used the opportunity to address far deeper matters. First he asked for a coin. The significance of this small detail is often overlooked. It probably means that Jesus himself did not carry coins because, like a good Jew, he would not want to associate with anything which bore a human image, still less the image of one who was ranked as a god. So when we imagine this scene, we might well imagine Jesus looking at the coin in a disdainful way, distancing himself from it and all that it represents. As Tom Wright puts it,

> We watch the scene as Jesus takes the coin from them, like someone being handed a dead rat. He looks at it with utter distaste. 'Whose is this . . . image? And who is it that gives himself an inscription like that?'[2]

What the Bible does not tell us is the colour of the Pharisees' faces as they say, 'It is Caesar's!' It must have been really galling; their strategy having been to get Jesus to confront the Romans. But Jesus' battle was not with the Romans. 'Let Caesar have what is his,' he said – and we can imagine him tossing the coin back to them. Then, as they walked away he might have added, 'but don't forget to give to God the things that are God's'. The saying is not about a separation of Church and state, God's realm and the realm of earthly powers. Rather, it concerns the distinction between the apparent value of what we call wealth and the lasting worth of the things of God. It is a distinction that lies at the heart of many issues we have been considering in relation to humility.

In the autumn of 2008, the financial system of the world fell first into chaos and then into crisis. Some people panicked. Others learnt how to make personal gain at the expense of the system as a whole. The subtle equilibrium between trust and greed that had held the market in the dynamic of continued growth for so many years was severely damaged, possibly even broken. People were quick to blame 'greedy bankers'. But bankers are bound to be greedy, not because they are bankers but because they are human beings. Jesus sought to free people from the power of sin, and he showed the rich young man one way of coping with greed. Give it all away! You may not like that particular method. But if you don't, you will have to find another.

Our greed does not just evaporate. Rather, it gets fixated. We can be acquisitive about just about anything. Think of some of the extraordinary things that people intentionally collect and the range of items that accumulate in modern homes as clutter. But the greatest snare for our greedy impulses is money itself. The love of money is strangely powerful.

Observing our own emotional and spiritual responses when the economy takes a downturn can be salutary. We take a quiet yet worldly pleasure when the economy is growing. We know that when the tide comes in, all the boats in the harbour rise effortlessly on it and that, as the economy in general grows, so our own financial position improves. When the tide goes out, we are tempted to lapse into fear and panic because we realize that our personal wealth is slowly but surely slipping away. The suffering, of course, falls unevenly. Some lose jobs, some lose their homes; some find that either their own investments or those of their pension fund do not open the door to the kind of retirement for which they are hoping. Our worldly hopes take quite a battering when the economy goes into recession. We have been encouraged to invest in the myth of relentless economic growth: the perpetually rising economic tide. We look forward to the increased personal wealth and leisure that we have seen others enjoy. It is not yet clear whether the credit crunch and all that flows from it will deconstruct the myth of relentless economic growth. But we learn something about our souls, something about ourselves, something about the sincerity and depth of our discipleship, when we see ourselves reacting with such concern and dismay to the prospect of a lifestyle which, while less affluent than we had hoped, remains, in global terms, amazingly privileged.

The reality is that, despite the economic downturn and recession, those in the west will continue to enjoy a lifestyle and level of comfort and security that their grandparents could hardly imagine, never mind their contemporaries in many other parts of the world. While we are rightly concerned for those for whom a recession means that they experience real poverty, for many of the world's wealthier inhabitants the recent economic strictures might be the God-given opportunity to discover that there is more to the meaning of life than the leisured enjoyment of riches or the mere absence of poverty. Indeed, both the gospel message and Christian experience suggest that the flame of the gospel is more readily extinguished by wealth than by poverty. It might be that, like a nocturnal tumble down a dark staircase, a fall in the market might be a wake-up call to the virtue and practice of Christian humility. Certainly humility struggles to get a look-in when our imaginations are captured by endless economic growth. No one is humbled by becoming richer whether by hard work or by, say, winning the lottery. Mere luck offers us no spiritual formation. Success is not much better. 'Nothing succeeds like success' they say. The reality, perhaps, is that when we are caught up in a cycle of success, we tend to get a bit intoxicated by it. We forget to contemplate the stars or to wonder at the beauty and fragility of the environment. We fail to attend to those things that might help us to discover our true significance and smallness. Like good luck and wealth, success is a poor educator because it dupes us into forgetting our limits. Humility, on the other hand, is the virtue that helps us understand and live with our limits.

In his book, *What Is the Point of Being a Christian?*, Timothy Radcliffe included a chapter about the African idea of 'ubuntu' which stresses the communal nature of human existence: 'It is because we are that I am.' It is significant that he writes about humility in the same chapter, specifically in a section entitled 'Learning to say "We".'[3] To explain the power of humility, he comments on Jesus' story in Luke's Gospel of the rich and successful farmer who needs to take down his barns and build bigger ones to store his crops befeore taking his ease (Luke 12.16–20). This is the man who sees life as the occasion to 'eat, drink and be merry'. The point here is not that we should neglect to celebrate living, enjoy life and delight in its pleasures, but that there is a great deal wrong in understanding our lives as the opportunity to store up material pleasures for ourselves. Such an approach distracts us from the Christlike way of passionate humility. It is the way of greed. That it should go together with arrogance and other forms of bad pride should not surprise us. As we live and learn, mostly by semi-conscious processes of habituation, so the vices, like the virtues, cluster together in the human character. That is one reason why we must be open to learning humility. The hope of becoming humble will never be satisfied but it will pull us away from more harmful forms of personal development – such as becoming wealthy or consuming disproportionate quantities of our planet's resources.

One person who learnt how to move from the world of money and gain to that of discipleship and generosity was Zacchaeus (Luke 19.1–10). For him it was the effort of simply trying to see Jesus that made all the difference because it led to Jesus seeing him and inviting himself home to share a meal. Significantly, we do not know much at all about what was said at the meal, but it cannot have been of the 'blah, blah' variety because the occasion was an absolute turning point. He changed his ways and gave back all he had gained by greed, returning it with fourfold interest. Another was Levi, who left his comfortable, money-making job, for the arduous but ultimately far more rewarding path of being a disciple of Jesus; in the process adopting the new name of Matthew. The suddenness of that decision, echoing that of the fishermen who left their boats, is hard for us to identify with. We don't know whether or not he would have grieved for the familiar routines of work and the financial benefits that came with it. But it is rare for people to look in the rear-view mirror of life without some pang of nostalgia. The call of Levi and his response as Matthew is indicative of the liberating demands of all Christian calling and discipleship. Following Jesus involves working with our attitude to possessions and to money. The advice to the rich young man is not advice that everyone could or should take literally. But it does challenge us to think about how much of our soul we invest in our things, and how greatly we rely on our wealth, modest and negligible as we naturally think it is, for our sense of who we are as well as our wellbeing and security.

Abundance or Scarcity?

The Christian gospel provides us with a lens onto God which reveals that the heart of God is to be found in endless self-giving. This truth has in many ways caught the imagination of the theological world in recent years. The subject of gift and giving is given endless theological scrutiny in the academy; scrutiny which it can take and reward, so robust, subtle and profound is the grace of God. This in turn has issued in a powerful new understanding of the grandeur and dignity, the *almightiness* if you will, of God which is located not in raw power, perfection or distance, but in God's expansive resourcefulness and endless generosity. This is the belief and teaching that the grace of God is absolutely limitless; it is often spoken of as the abundance or superabundance of God.

Abundance theology and Christian discipleship are drawn together in Samuel Wells' book, *God's Companions*. Introducing the idea, Wells talks about three Gospel stories, the miracle of water into wine at Cana (John 2), the meeting of Jesus with the

Samaritan woman at the well (John 4) and the miracle of the loaves and fishes (John 6). Or, as he calls them, the stories of 'too much wine', 'too much water' and 'too much bread'.[4] In each case the story begins with a crisis of scarcity, in each case there is an exchange with Jesus, and in each case the end result is an excess of what was scarce in the first place. As Wells clarifies when expounding the water into wine story, it is not a story of water purification but it is a story in which the inadequacy of fallen creation in general and Israel in particular is 'transformed by the generosity of God'.

> It is a story of enough becoming not enough becoming too much. It is a parable of the person and work of Christ. This is the story of the Gospel: God in Christ overwhelms his despondent people by giving them far more than they need.[5]

Wells, and theologians like him such as David Ford, give a high priority to this doctrine of the abundance of God and the endless generosity of God's grace.[6] God is seen as having an eternal and limitless capacity *to give* and this leads on to what one might call 'abundance thinking'. It is the mantra of Wells' book: 'God gives his people everything they need to worship him, to be his friends, and to eat with him.'[7] However, the life of the Church on the ground in the parishes and dioceses is animated by a very different train of thought. Indeed it is often all but dominated by 'scarcity thinking'. The kind of thinking that is convinced that there is not enough resource to do all that we can, should or could. This is the kind of thinking that responds to a great idea with a heavy heart, 'If only things were different, then we would do it.' Contrast this with what Wells has to say about the story of the five barley loaves and two little fish.

Jesus takes, gives thanks, and shares: eucharistic actions that embody appropriate ways for disciples to engage with the 'too much' that Jesus offers. Stretching the disciples' and the people's imaginations, Jesus gives the people as much as they want: everything they need.[8]

When a bishop decided to challenge such 'scarcity thinking', he entitled the paper where he set out his position, *Six Months' Wages*. To many, it was an obscure reference, but the intention was to draw them into this same story. For when Jesus asks the disciple Philip how he thinks the crowd might be fed, he replies, 'Six months' wages would not buy enough bread for each of them to get a little' (John 6.7). The bishop was trying to nudge people towards a glimpse of the glory of 'abundance mentality' which is characteristic of authentic Christian discipleship. In the realpolitik of the synods and councils of the Church, where budgets have to be made and where expenditure cannot exceed income for many years without ruin, prudence is often the inherited and unquestioned form of wisdom. In such a context, the theological voice which speaks of superabundance is not the easiest one for a gathering to heed, or even respect. Theological principle is often dismissed as the voice of the ivory tower idealist and contrasted with the compelling power of down-to-earth, practical 'common sense'. The sad truth is that a fundamental theological decision has to be made, which, like all such decisions, might fly in the face of common sense, reason and worldly wisdom. It is this: does God give plenty or does God give not quite enough? Are we going to think 'abundance' or 'scarcity'? Are we doing ordinary economics here or 'God's business'?

The fundamental problem here is one of faithful imagination. It seems to me that unless God is cruel and mean, God must provide all the resources needful to allow us to fulfil our calling to share in mission. Passionate humility involves making a commitment to trust in the abundance of God and to believe and act as if we believe that there is plenty of money, talent, time for mission and ministry. Like all good faith, it believes what it does not yet see and acts on its beliefs. For the Barefoot Disciple, the problem is not that the resources are not there, it is that they have not yet been spotted or liberated. It is odd to put it this way, but we cannot even imagine what is before our eyes. As Wells asserts, 'The disciples, endlessly, fail the test of imagination . . .'[9] It's true. Even Andrew, who spots the boy with loaves and fish, sighs, 'But what are they among so many people?' (John 6.9). That small phrase is in danger of becoming the strapline of the Church today. And while that is bad enough, it gets worse. Not only do we fail to believe in God's abundance, we also find ways perversely to stand in its way. This is the challenge that sits at the heart of what we often call Christian *stewardship*. The emphasis in this is often on financial giving and the need to get more money from more people to balance the parochial and diocesan budgets and fund new work. At best, that is a very partial way of looking at it. The real battle here is between the abundance and the scarcity mentalities. This is not a new problem. It runs through the Gospels. Jesus represents and offers 'excessive grace'. Just about everyone else stands for something a little more sensible. There are some, however, who have at least an inkling of what Jesus stands for and is talking about.

Wells sees the decisive clash of mentalities taking place at Bethany where Jesus is anointed by Mary (John 12). We have visited this story before, seeing the anointing as a formative experience. Now it comes into focus as an act of generosity. It is based on the abundance mentality that we have been discussing, but some who witness it do so through the economic lens of scarcity thinking. They speak of the cost, the 300 denarii; that's a year's wages, never mind six months'! They begin to think of the poor, wrongly connecting an act of celebratory generosity with the systematic oppression and exploitation and ongoing moral blindness that not only creates poverty but also holds people in it. All this turns the heart of one of the disciples away from the glimpse of heaven seen in Jesus and towards the lonely darkness that awaits him. As Wells notes, 'Immediately after this scene Judas went to the chief priests to betray Jesus – ironically, for money.'[10]

The central economic and spiritual problem for the Church today, though it is rarely identified as such, is not the dominating question of what are we to do when money is so short, but this one: 'What are we to do with our belief that God is endlessly generous and supplies all our needs so abundantly that there is an excess of what we need?' This is, to be sure, the theologian's question. But it is not a question that should be locked away in an ivory tower. Rather, it is the question that comes from serious, sustained meditation on the nature and mission of God and the life, death and resurrection of Jesus. Such reflection reminds us that God is not the item at the end of the agenda, but the reason why we have an agenda at all. It affirms that Jesus Christ, the word, or *logos*, made flesh, is the principle that must order our priorities and connect our theory and our practice. It is only if we do this that we get beyond the 'blah, blah'; the hot air of our own self-important meanness. It is not as if there is some other more compelling reality than God which we must attend to first so that in the end we might engage with things of ultimate value. God does not sit on a pinnacle at the top of Abraham Maslow's hierarchy of needs. Rather, God in Christ represents and reveals the spiritual–material values that give us meaning and purpose. This is why the theological approach to discipleship, based on adult learning, humility and 'abundance thinking', emphasizes giving and generosity. It reframes our approach to stewardship so that it is less about persuading people that they have a duty to give a little more, and more about helping people to realize how much they have to give. There *is* an abundance available. The only problem is that when we see what is to hand, we fear, with Andrew, that it will not be enough.

Generosity of Spirit

Our focus in this chapter has been on *words* – we are too generous with them; *possessions* – we are too dependent on them; and *money* – we are generally confused about it. True generosity, however, is not about what we do with this or that thing but is a disposition of who we are which is reflected in the way in which we deal with all kinds of things and all kinds of people. At the end of the day it is 'generosity of spirit' that matters. When people describe us as having this quality, we should perhaps allow ourselves a brief moment of good pride . . . and then think of three people whom we ourselves might praise and encourage for the same quality. Living generously is an 'across the board', 'whole of life', matter. There is almost no end to what generous people can find to give: time, kindness, space, material goods, charity, empathy, patience and so on. On the other hand, there is a short and unhappy list of words which apply to those who have not yet learnt the joy of giving: mean, niggardly, miserly, greedy, grudging, selfish and exploiting. Just to list these words demonstrates what sad lives we can end up living if we fail to learn how to be generous.

Abundance thinking generates both humility and hope. If you believe that the resources are there but that they are not yet apparent, you set yourself and others the interesting challenge not of creating them, but of creating the context in which they can and will be offered. Sometimes this will involve asking, and maybe asking big. Presumably Andrew did actually ask the little boy with the packed lunch if it was okay to share it. I wonder how he responded. Maybe we should try to picture his face. It's an expression which good Christian ministers will be familiar with because they will often ask people if they would like to share what they have got. Thinking all this through makes me want to suggest that helping others to share and to give needs to come up much higher on our all too churchy 'to do' lists. Creating the friendly, courteous, supportive environment in which people can actually offer their gifts with modesty but still engage their passion for the kingdom is a far more important ministerial task than we usually think. It calls for the level 5 leadership that Jim Collins has identified and which we discussed in Chapter 3. Leadership which combines humility with passion will not only make space for the gifts and talents of others, it will actively seek to draw them out. Good ministerial leadership will facilitate generous living not because there is a need to balance the accounts but because giving, like humility and learning, is intrinsic to discipleship. None of these are extras; they are the essence of Christlike living. That is why we need to get humility not only into our head and heart, but also into our bones. When we are people of passionate humility we also become people open to learning, whom others think of as having generosity of spirit.

The story of forgiveness in Luke 15 is often called the story of the prodigal son. However, the key point is not the son's wasteful prodigality but the father's endless generosity: a generosity that naturally incorporates the gift of forgiveness. That story has often been called the gospel within the Gospel. If it is re-titled as 'the generous father' it comes close to justifying that title. The truth is that the ways of God are much less sensible and prudent than we dare to think. That is not to say that they are not reasonable; rather, it is to assert that there is a divine reason which is different, and that as we learn it we become differently wise. That 'reason' or *logos* was made real in Jesus and is an alternative to worldly wisdom which focuses on calculations of cost and projects that aim at 'growth'. The beginning and ending of God, and Christ, is generosity. When human beings begin to think in that way, there is a profound and three-dimensional transformation of people and institutions.

One Sunday, the reading set for a service at which I was preaching began with the word, 'Then'. It is an odd place to begin. '*Then* the leaders of ancestral houses made their freewill offerings' (1 Chronicles 29.6). In the sermon I let the congregation know what it was that had occasioned this making of freewill offerings. It was very simple. The King himself had just set an example of giving. Giving is not a difficult or complex matter. It is a way of living that people don't need explaining to them, though they often do need an example to follow. Following in the way of giving is the primary calling of the Barefoot Disciple. That is, we are to follow the one who 'emptied himself, taking the form of a slave' (Philippians 2.7): Jesus, the One who definitively connected generosity with humility. It is a connection at the heart of discipleship. It is a connection which, in Christ, cannot be broken because it reflects the nature of God: the humble creator, forgiver and inspirer; the One for whom to exist is to give. Entering into generosity is integral to growing in passionate humility both because it is the passionate side of our personality that is engaged when we give, however modestly, and because true giving involves passing on what we ourselves have received as gift.

Often the questions of motivation and reward come up when we think about giving. There are some who cannot imagine the possibility of pure generosity – just giving because it is a good thing to give. Similarly, there are those who cannot believe in the possibility that the development of virtue is something which is of value in its own right. This has often been a problem for Christian thinkers, who see that a focus on virtue might be bringing in egocentrism by the back door; that it focuses on the self rather than the neighbour. This can be a subtle business, as we saw Michael Ramsey note earlier when he spoke of the danger of half-conscious self-congratulation.[11] As Jennifer Herdt has put it: 'A person who aspires to the virtue of gratitude will act not only out of gratitude itself but also out of the motivation of seeing herself as a person who acts gratefully.'[12] What is true for gratitude is even truer for generosity. Surely, we exclaim, generosity cannot be true generosity if part of the motivation is the pride that the giver takes in thinking of themselves as generous. Such motivation is quite incompatible with humility. Such a line of thought takes us straight to everyone's favourite story of giving, the story of the widow's mite (Luke 21.1–4). We admire her gift because we cannot imagine that giving it makes her feel that she is better than us. But maybe we misread the story. The point is not that she gives modestly but that she gives excessively – 'all she had to live on' (Luke 21.4). The truth is that we have no idea what she thought she was doing or whether she took pride in her giving. We like the story because we read it to say that small gifts can be generous. They can, especially when they consist of *all* that you have.

In any case, our concern is not with the motivation or generosity of others, nor with the way in which others judge us, but with the difference that our own actions make. Virtue thinking seems to be inward-looking because it is concerned with the development of character and the acquisition of good habits of thought and action. But the real power of this approach, and the reason why humility is the virtue of virtues, is that it is concerned with real long-term consequences. Generosity, whether great or modest, can always be self-regarding. We can even quietly congratulate ourselves on being 'anonymous' and preen our invisible feathers while others gasp at the magnanimity and modesty of the unknown donor in their midst. However, we must not let this psycho-ethical knot distract us from the path of seeking to be the kind of person who, whether admired or not, whether feeling good or not, will, by dint of habit, tend to do the kind of thing that characterizes the kingdom of God and which reflects the life and teaching of Jesus. The point about humility is its selfless respect for reality. The truly generous person, the person who combines generosity with humility, is not aiming to be generous but to make a difference to others.

All of which takes us back to a question that troubled us right at the beginning of the book: 'Can we make ourselves humble?' The answer is vital for any virtue spirituality. It is 'Yes and no': 'Yes, we can intentionally cultivate humility by engaging in self-forgetful practices which are likely to foster humility in our character'; 'No, we can never say that such humility as we have developed is of our own making.' The humble person knows that they are themself a gift and that such virtue as they have acquired is something that they have been given.

A genuinely humble person is a grateful and unself-conscious giver. Can they take pride in that? This time it is 'No and yes'. No, if the form of pride is self-congratulatory conceit. Yes, if it is good pride, because the person who is proud in a good way knows what is good and delights in it. Rewards do not matter to the passionately humble. What matters to them is the kingdom of God. A genuinely humble person does not need to dress their generosity up with false modesty by saying, 'It was the least I could do.' The widow who gave her mite was making a relatively small donation but it was all she had. That's both generous and humble. Humility, it cannot be stressed enough, has nothing to do with coming out with words which are intended to persuade others that we are not taking pride in our achievements. It is about being honest, generous, open and engaged with the world as it is transfigured and transformed into the kingdom of God.

Notes

1. Harries, *Is There a Gospel for the Rich?*, p. 1.
2. Wright, *Matthew for Everyone*, p. 87.
3. Radcliffe, *What Is the Point of Being a Christian?*, pp. 132–42.
4. Wells, *God's Companions*, pp. 18–23.
5. Wells, *God's Companions*, p. 19.
6. Ford, *Christian Wisdom* and *The Shape of Living, passim*.
7. Wells, *God's Companions*, p. 1 and *passim*.
8. Wells, *God's Companions*, p. 22.
9. Wells, *God's Companions*, p. 23.
10. Wells, *God's Companions*, p. 24.
11. Page 36 above.
12. Herdt, *Putting On Virtue*, p. 345.

CHAPTER 9

Bodily Spirituality

Knowing that I was working on humility, a friend gave me a copy of an article from the scholarly journal *Modern Theology*. The author, Norman Wirzba, argues that we fail properly to understand our place in the world and our indebtedness to others, and that these failures are best understood in terms of what he calls 'rebellion against humility'. He goes on to say that:

Humility is central to human life because it is through a humble attitude that we most fully approximate our true condition as creatures dependent on others, daily implicated in the life and death-wielding ways of creation, all together sustained by the gifts of our Creator. It is in terms of humility that we express our understanding that we do not stand alone or through our own effort, but live through the sacrifices and kindnesses of others.[1]

For Wirzba, humility is the quality that helps us to appreciate what he calls our *interdependent creatureliness*. There is a social aspect to this. It is through humility that we grasp our need for other people and appreciate that social life is not an 'extra' but fundamental to being human. Genuine humility always takes us to the third person, to the ever-expanding circle of the 'we', a sense of 'us' that does not need a 'them' to bolster or vindicate itself. The word 'humility' refers us to our *interdependence* and reminds us that independence is an arrogant myth. But Wirzba goes beyond that.

When the question of what it means to be human is raised, we usually address it in terms of what it means to be *distinctively* human. The answers are often found in the realm of the higher intellectual functions: only humans have consciousness or language. Or in the realm of the emotions: only humans love. Reflecting on humility suggests that we recognize that this approach is so laden with danger that it is better to try to address the issue of what we have in common. Humility helps us realize not only that we are human beings, but also to recognize the animal side of our nature, our creatureliness. This is not always welcome, as Charles Darwin discovered when he proposed the theory of natural selection. It is essential, however, if we are fully to understand ourselves and each other. Humility suggests that when it comes to our relationship with the animal kingdom, it is *connectedness*, not our distinctiveness, that is the most important consideration.

What is common, not only to humanity, but to all creatures? It is a good question and it would take a long time to construct an adequate answer. All the sciences can offer something. Physics reminds us that we are all subject to gravity and the laws of time and space; chemistry, that we are all made of the same chemical ingredients; biology tells us that there is an enormous amount of overlap between our DNA and that of, say, a cucumber, never mind a gorilla. We are profoundly interconnected and interdependent. We are all part of the same physical universe, the same ecosystem. If it were not so, we would not exist. How strange, then, that we put so much effort into seeking out what makes us different, special, superior, whether as a social group, a race, a gender or as individuals. This is not the way of humility. It is the way of superiority which, as Wirzba emphasizes, expresses itself in the arrogant desire to take control by harnessing all the powers of technology to achieve its intended results. The way of humility takes us in another direction altogether. Here the desire is not control, and the means is not technology. The moral ambition is, rather, connectedness. It was E. M. Forster who most famously made this point in his novel, *Howards End*.

> Only connect the prose and the passion, and both will be exalted, and human love will be seen at its highest. Live in fragments no longer. Only connect, and the beast and the monk, robbed of the isolation that is life to either, will die.[2]

That summary of Margaret Schlegel's sermon to Henry Wilcox could stand as a manifesto for the project of passionate humility. It primarily refers to the intra-connectedness of the facets of the human personality, but it can speak to other levels of our condition too. Today we are beginning to wake up to the need to understand not only the interconnectedness of all human life but of all life, indeed the whole of creation. While this often seems a fresh aspect of our consciousness, it is far from new. It is a theme which comes across very powerfully through the lives of saints like Cuthbert of Lindisfarne and Francis of Assisi: for instance, in the stories of otters drying the feet of Cuthbert after a prayer vigil in the sea and Francis taming the wild wolf of Gubbio and reconciling it with the terrorized people of the town. True humility always seeks to break down barriers and to communicate across difference and diversity. True humility always tries to connect the prose and the passion. True humility always strives to engage the ministry of reconciliation in its widest possible sense. For God did not seek to redeem or reconcile from afar. Rather, it was that '*in Christ* God was reconciling the world to himself' (2 Corinthians

5.19). God's method is not to control; it is always to connect. This is why loving humility is, as Dostoyevsky put it, 'a terrible force'. It is God's grace in down-to-earth action.

Humanimals

In 2009, Durham Cathedral hosted an exhibition of the work of South African sculptor Jane Alexander. It was a collaborative venture with the University's Institute of Advanced Studies which, that year, focused on the theme of 'Being Human'. While the centrepiece of the exhibition was Alexander's 'Bom Boys', there were also several of her 'humanimals' on display. The observer is never sure whether these hybrid forms are more human or bird, more animal than human. They are federated creatures, as it were, made up of bits and pieces and formed into a whole by the artist not to suggest a new type of organism, but to blur the boundaries in our imaginations which divide between 'us' and 'them'. That, at least, is my reading of them. There is something both monstrous and pathetic about many of her works, for Alexander is commenting not only on the human condition and what Wirzba would call interdependency, but also on what is routinely called the 'dehumanizing' impact of apartheid. This comes across even more strongly in the 'Bom Boys', nine diminutive figures that seem like abandoned children. Some are fully clothed but some are naked, though their faces are all masked or obscured in some way. Their eyes are moist but they speak to us less of victimhood and more of ambiguity. They are both victims and aggressors and they arouse a range of emotions, drawing us into the agony of lives framed and formed by inhuman boundaries.

The hope was that the humanimals and Bom Boys would inhabit the Galilee Chapel keeping company with the tomb of the Venerable Bede and Joseph Pyrz's contemporary sculpture of the Blessed Virgin Mary. The Cathedral was being invited to push the boundaries a bit here. But that was inevitable. Jane Alexander's work invites us to recognize that the drawing of boundaries is not a very adequate way of coming to the truth of things. Boundaries might be fine ways of managing difficult situations and bringing some provisional order in a chaotic environment, but they also have a terrible power. Not only do they frame our experience, they also limit what we see and think and feel. Boundaries have implications in terms of freedom, identity and justice. The architects of apartheid understood the power of boundaries and made them their most powerful tool. We know the story. First human beings were divided into different 'racial' categories. Next they were treated differently and given different rights. Then they were segregated by the Group Areas Act which divided the country into different townships and areas deemed to be fit for members of the different racial groups. Few testimonies from the apartheid era in South Africa are more powerful than those of people who were removed from their homes and dumped in another neighbourhood and left to make the best of it.

Unwittingly, the Jane Alexander exhibition in Durham Cathedral was augmented by a testimony to this boundary-creating mentality. In order to protect the gaze of schoolchildren from the humanimals and the Bom Boys when they were visiting Bede's tomb, a makeshift wall was constructed. As the Galilee Chapel has two doors, one was used for the exhibition and the other for school parties. Only one entrance has a ramp, however, so those needing to use it had to use the children's entrance and then make their way through a specially created door in the specially created wall. We had unwittingly, and with the best possible motives, reconstructed an 'us' and 'them' situation. It takes more to get beyond this tendency to create boundaries, this 'apartheid of the mind', than we sometimes like to imagine. The Venerable Bede and his pilgrims were in one area, Jane Alexander's sculptures and their visitors in another. Pyrz's Blessed Virgin Mary, however, was on the exhibition side of the wall. As the original Barefoot Disciple, in touch with the earth, with the poor, with danger and uncertainty and in solidarity with those who have seen loved ones tortured or killed and have held their dead bodies, Mary was keeping deep fellowship. As the Dean put it in an essay in a publication which accompanied the exhibition:

> I see Jane Alexander's figures as keeping good company with Mary. Their thought-provoking juxtaposition points to the one whom Christianity calls 'the Last Adam', the true human being who took our condition and entered into its contradictions and pain in order to bring about the redemption of the world.[3]

Maybe the Venerable Bede himself, whose entombed bones were screened away from the figures, would have approved of the exhibition but been disappointed with the screen. It was Bede, after all, who passed on the stories of Cuthbert and the animals with warm approval. For instance, he tells us of when Cuthbert rebuked some ravens for tearing straw from the roof of the visitors' house and using it for their own nests. 'Three days later one of a pair of them returned and, finding Cuthbert digging, stood before him, with feathers outspread and head bowed low to its feet in sign of grief.' Cuthbert accepted the gesture and invited them to return. They did so, bearing a gift of pig's lard. This in turn occasioned a profound spiritual reversal. Cuthbert was no longer preaching *to* the birds but extolling their example: 'What care should not men take' he would say, 'to cultivate obedience and humility when the very birds hasten to wash away their faults of pride by prayers, tears and gifts.'[4]

Being In Touch

Not long into my training for ordained ministry, it occurred to me to wonder whether there was one primary, fundamental, pastoral issue. I decided that if there was, it was loneliness. It was visiting a man who said that he looked to his budgie for company that decided me. When still in the early months of my first post as a vicar, I made the point at a 'Churches Together' meeting when we were discussing social responsibility. 'It must be the task of the church to work for a society where no one is lonely,' I announced, with all the naïve pomposity of the new kid on the block. People were not convinced. They wanted something with more of a political edge than that. Later someone told me that he found my suggestion amusing. That, in turn, made *me* feel lonely. I had failed to communicate. This failure is common and yet I remain convinced that it is a missionary task to build bridges of communication and to wage spiritual warfare against all the powers and forces that would make people lonely. Sometimes the Church does do this. I have come to see both pastoral work and community engagement as a strategic campaign in God's long-term war against human loneliness. Bereavement, loss, illness, ongoing suffering – all these are problematic. But all are far worse when compounded by loneliness. For, just as the body can be the door to humility, so loneliness can be the doorway to shame, guilt and despair. It is loneliness that twists the knife of grief.

Reading Norman Wirzba's article suggests to me that there is a double connection to be made between the problem of loneliness, the virtue of humility and the practice of pastoral care. The connection is this. Wirzba suggests that the only sort of person who can be genuinely humble is the person who is profoundly and significantly *in touch*. When we are in touch we are communicating, that is giving and receiving, but also recognizing our creatureliness *and* our connectedness with the earth itself. It is this bodily in-touchness that gives us what Wirzba calls 'an opening into humility'.

> As humans we are tactile beings immersed and embedded in a world of bodies. It is in terms of the vast and deep memberships of creation, what ecologists call 'webs of interdependence', that we derive our nurture and inspiration, our very being. We live *through* others and could not possibly live alone.[5]

Taking humility seriously, then, does not prevent us taking ourselves seriously, but it does prevent us seeing ourselves as isolated and abstracted individuals. Adapting a famous slogan, the humble person might say neither, 'I think therefore I am' nor even, 'I touch therefore I am', but, '*I am in touch* therefore I am'.

Being in touch is at the heart of the pastoral ministry of the Church, which is a ministry shared by both lay and ordained disciples. Sincere, sensitive, practical care is always humble and often humbling. Being in touch can take many forms. Pastoral wit, experience and imagination are well deployed when this challenge is faced creatively. Sometimes a phone call does the trick. I am still moved when I receive a phone call on my birthday from the parish where I was once the incumbent, even if it takes the form of an answerphone message. On other occasions, only written, possibly handwritten, communication will meet the need. Sometimes it is good to send a card, but cards are not right for every occasion and there are limits to the number that can be sent. To my surprise, I have found occasions in ministry when text messaging proved the best way of being in touch. It can be a way of expressing vigilance of thought and prayer without breaking in on someone's time and attention. Email is an efficient form of communication but its capacity to transmit emotion is regularly underestimated. We are all learning of its power to transmit, exaggerate and create feeling through trial and error, and most users will have been on both the giving and receiving ends of emails which cause upset and aggravate loneliness because they were sent in haste. But even email can be a means of pastoral care, of being in touch when it makes a big difference. I was on the receiving end of daily email support from a friend in another continent while a close relative was dying. It was not only comforting to know that a candle was burning thousands of miles away, it was also helpful and unobtrusive to get gentle suggestions and supportive thoughts just when my own energy was dropping and my spirit flagging. While all these methods and media can genuinely communicate care, a different quality of engagement is achieved by an actual, physical, real-time *visit*.

The dynamics of humility are integral to the practice of pastoral visiting. To visit a family, or maybe a lonely widow or widower, in order to prepare for a funeral is often to walk into an environment so fractured and disconnected that the spectre of eternal loneliness is fearfully close. Few can effectively break the ice of disconnection in these situations without some form of physical touch, even if it is only a lingering handshake in the doorway. More often, hands are held, forearms or shoulders gently touched. Eye-contact matters too. It is a kind of non-physical touch – visual touch perhaps. People need to see and be seen in the same moment, the same contact. But such touch, such contact, is far more than a metaphor or an expression. It is companionship and accompaniment; it is the essence of basic human solidarity. It works in reverse too. Sometimes those who reach out to those in distress find themselves being held. This has always come as something of a surprise to me and it can be a challenge to remain calmly and positively in the company of a stranger who is literally clinging on. There is simple, genuine, vulnerable reality in the need to hold and be held. Humble, pastoral hospitality, expressed, perhaps paradoxically, in visiting, can both feel and meet this need.

Christian ministry always involves mutuality. It never involves merely meeting the needs of others. It is two-way traffic. Ann Morisy is highly critical of what she calls the 'needs meeting' approach which often extends to community engagement and social welfare projects. A worthy aim can never be merely to impact on 'them'. It has to be about creating a new 'us'. 'The radical, missionary activity of the Church cannot, like liberal, secular social policy, aim at the transformation of the poor . . . the aim must be the transformation of the secure, the well-meaning and the well-endowed of the world.'[6] Her alternative to 'meeting needs' or 'doing good' is to enter into the cascade of grace that begins to flow when people seek not to provide for others, but to 'enter into a struggle for the well-being of others'. At this point she begins to open up a distinction between participating as a volunteer worker on a social project and entering into the same work as one who sees it as an expression of discipleship that always involves vulnerability and openness to learning. So within her vision of engagement with the poor and vulnerable (let us not say poor and needy) is a deepening of discipleship, not simply an expression of it.

> [Such] experience of discipleship provokes a deeper awareness of personal sin and recognition of our (the respectable!) complicity in sinful systems. Discipleship ceases to be understood as 'good works and meeting needs'. Rather discipleship fosters growth of a humility and recognition of inadequacy, both

personal and corporate, and on occasion, it is about having one's heart broken.[7]

True discipleship takes us to the limit of competency and capacity and well outside our personal comfort zone. Indeed, it is in such heart-breaking and soul-forming territory that discipleship flourishes into ministry because it is only here that we can be properly aware that ministry is always mutual. This is regularly the experience of those who have ministered, as Jesus commanded, to the sick, the dying, those in prison and the poor. To take a very simple example: I have never been able to look forward very positively to celebrating Communion services in residential homes. Nonetheless, this ministerial duty has given me countless tiny intimations of grace, moments of human warmth and genuine love, strange insights into the meaning of a biblical phrase or story, new glimpses into the significance of the sacrament. All these and more have been among the blessings. Often on these occasions any participants who have been churchgoers all their lives, or maybe at some formative stage in their younger years, join in the more familiar and memorable words. They remember the words, but have forgotten that they should leave them to the priest to say. It is therefore with a blend of remembering and forgetfulness which is utterly truthful to the human condition that they say 'This is my body', or mutter, 'Do this in remembrance of me'. Sometimes, at the very end, they rightly, as I realize now, join in the words of the blessing: 'The peace of God which passes all understanding keep your hearts and minds . . .'

It is only when barriers are broken that the graceful mutuality of ministry can be released.

But Dust

Every Ash Wednesday the Church gives us the opportunity to get in touch with reality in a way that is both real and symbolic. The practice of 'ashing', or daubing an ashen cross on the forehead, is intended to bring us down to earth. It is simultaneously a call to humility and to repentance. It encourages us to make a change of mind and heart and to reorient our lives to God. As the ash goes onto the forehead, so the minister says: 'Remember that you are dust and to dust you will return. Turn from sin and be faithful to Christ.' Remember that you are dust! It is a quotation from Genesis where God expels Adam and Eve from the Garden of Eden. The curse of humankind inflicts struggle and toil before an eventual return to dust. The Ash Wednesday ritual says to us that we should think neither too highly nor too lowly of our-selves, but that we should always remember our connectedness with, our participation in, the dusty earth. Even earlier in Genesis, the first human was named 'Adam', the name itself meaning something like 'earthling', creature of the earth. As countless science fiction writers have suggested, this is how an alien would think of us and name us. It is the name of creatures of dust, of the earth; it is the name of our common humanity, our basic humility.

When he wrote up his experiences on 11 September 2001, Rowan Williams called his little book, *Writing in the Dust*.[8] There was a lot of dust about that day. Much of it was the dust of build-ing rubble. But mixed in with it was stuff that takes to the air when flesh and blood and bone and hair are burnt. That's the trouble with dust. You don't know what it is made up of. All sorts of things blend in its powder. It's an uncomfortable, messy mix. Dust is the ultimate form of dirt. Anthropologists tell us that often it is just material that is in the wrong place. There is a place for everything, but when things are out of place they are dirt. When we have our hair cut we see this happening before our very eyes. One moment those hairs are our finery; the next, they are dirt. Hair on the floor has lost all meaning and dignity; even the smidgen of beauty it could once call its own is gone. Unlike hair, dust is always dirt. There is no good place for dust to be.

When we read Genesis 2 we discover that dust is not only our destiny, it is the stuff of which we are made. 'The Lord formed man from the dust of the earth.' It is our beginning as well as our end. When Job felt particularly dejected, he said that God formed him out of clay and protested against being returned to dust (Job 10.9). As well he might. The prospect does not flatter us. It does not tell us what we want to hear about our future. Dust represents the breakdown of order that we can perceive. Seen symbolically, dust prophesies the end of the cosmos in a long whimper of endless entropy. But Job's protest against the prospect of becoming dust came too late. Genesis 3 had already told us the story of disobedience and blame. That story led to the mythical punishments: the serpent is cursed to go on its belly and eat dust, the woman has her labour pains exacerbated, and the man is doomed to toiling the ground, which is itself cursed, for a mere crust. 'By the sweat of your face you shall eat bread until you return to the ground, for out of it you were taken; you are dust, and to dust you shall return' (Genesis 3.19). In that disturbing catalogue, the return to dust stands out as an empirical and eternal truth. As we give it our attention, so it takes us to the cemetery. 'As a father has compassion for his children, so the Lord has compassion on those that fear him. For he knows of what we are made; he remembers that we are but dust' (Psalm 103.13–14). These are well-worn words; words that have been seasoned at millions of gravesides in all kinds of weather. But one little word carries significance beyond all the others. It is the word, 'we'.

'*We* are but dust.' When it is said by the priest and heard by the mourners there is an unspoken and tacit recognition of solidarity. Graveside and basic it might be, but it is all the more real for that. For every funeral is a celebration of ordinary humility and common humanity. It is not only the deceased who are dust. We are all dust. That is both a sobering and a humbling thought. It brings home to us our creatureliness, our limits, our mortality.

When Jesus was dying on the cross, he cried out 'Eli, Eli, lema sabachthani?' That is, 'My God, my God, why have you forsaken me?' (Matthew 27.46, Mark 15.34). It is a heartfelt cry of despair and desolation. The words, however, are borrowed from the beginning of Psalm 22. The 31 verses of the Psalm take us on a journey from despair to desolation and on to absolute dereliction which reaches its nadir not at the end but in the middle:

> I am poured out like water,
> and all my bones are out of joint;
> my heart is like wax;
> it is melted within my breast;
> my mouth is dried up like a potsherd,
> and my tongue sticks to my jaws;
> you lay me in the dust of death. (Psalm 22.14, 15)

'The dust of death' is a powerful image of our destiny. But fundamental as dust is, we cannot understand our bodily spirituality without attending to either sin or the human mind. George Herbert once wrote this:

> Love bade me welcome, yet my soul drew back,
> Guiltie of dust and sinne.

'Dust' was a big word for Herbert. He used it to freight in all the biblical background that we have surveyed. For him, the individual person is a 'crumme of dust' destined to be 'crumbled into dust' at death.[9] In his poetry, the word 'dust' awakens us to the mortality that runs though our veins like dark blood. But he says more. According to Herbert we are guilty of dust *and sin*. Maybe he is alluding to original sin: the sin that we can neither commit nor avoid. There are many explanations and pictures of original sin in the old curiosity shop which is the history of theology and preaching. Few of them have been very convincing in recent generations. We are much more interested in saying, 'I'm okay, you're okay' or to find ways of sharing unconditional positive regard than in speculating about how it is that Adam's disobedience tumbles down the generations to me.

Original Sin

Seeking a passionately humble bodily spirituality demands that we think again about original sin, that aspect of who we are which we cannot eradicate and which drags us away from God. I want to suggest that this sin is not found in what we today call the flesh any more than it is in the peccadilloes of personal morality. Rather, the essence of sin is to be found in the nooks and crannies of the human mind; in particular, in the form of thinking that was demonstrated so spectacularly in apartheid South Africa and is so roundly challenged in Jane Alexander's species-bending creations. For sin is about denying the glory of God, denying the prodigality of God's grace, denying the wondrous creative and inspiring work of the Spirit which can illuminate and transfigure the whole of life and the whole of creation. The World Alliance of Reformed Churches famously denounced apartheid as a heresy. To bend language even more,

I would want to call it a 'sacrament of sin': an outward and visible sign of an inward and spiritual *disgrace*. To put it another way, apartheid, manifest and barbaric as it is, is not ultimately a cause but a symptom. It is the apartheid of the mind that really matters: that computer-like, binary, 'either–or' thinking that divides the world into 'us' and 'them'.

The end of apartheid remains something to celebrate. But it should not make us complacent, for apartheid was only a manifestation of a human tendency which is characteristic not only of our race but of each and every individual: the sinful habit of divisive and self-aggrandizing thought. It is second nature to us. Fortunately it is not first nature. Our first nature, like that of the animals, is far more contemplative and innocent. We might well be making spiritual progress if we become *more*, not less, like the animals; if we recognize more, not less, our common humanity; if we recognize more, not less, that we have far more in common with even the most heinous of sinners and criminals than we ever dare to admit. There but for the grace of God . . .

It is terribly difficult to put your finger on the nature of original sin but fantastically difficult to develop a mature understanding of what it means to be human without it. My suggestion here is that original sin is to be found precisely in the apartheid of the mind: dividing things into categories and then believing that the differences are more important than the commonalities. Regimes like apartheid, or the Indian caste system, attempt to squeeze God's seamless creation into the categories of the human mind. Full of fear and power, we project our intellectual limits onto the glorious diversity of God's creation, thereby making 'gods' of ourselves and oppressing others. People talk of the dehumanizing power of totalitarian regimes. But oppression is a less sure way of dehumanizing than self-aggrandizement. Turning the self into a god is the most dehumanizing of practices.

For when we do that, we lose sight of our own limits, we disconnect from others and the earth. We are lost in pride and loneliness because we are devoid of humility. The dehumanization of the powerful involves becoming captive to the practices of thought and imagination of which we are least aware. When it is at work, the apartheid of the mind rarely discloses its presence to its host (if I can put it that way). With diabolical cunning, the grossest, deepest sins of the self are disguised. The worst vices are presented as virtues and a culture is spun which is toxic to the distinctive Christian virtues, in particular humility. I don't want this to sound too portentous, but we need to be on the alert if we inhabit a context or culture where vices are assumed as normal behaviour and where virtues are regarded with distrust and suspicion. If this is our analysis we should at least grow in passion for God's kingdom, realizing that it is held at bay by the barriers that the apartheid of the mind seems to have endless capacity to construct.

Jesus said, 'Do not judge, so that you may not be judged. For with the judgement you make you will be judged' (Matthew 7.1–2). If we want to know what to make of the notion of original sin, maybe we need look no further than the artificial barriers and judgemental boundaries that make up the apartheid of our minds. They are difficult to spot at first. But as we grow in discernment we begin to see them for what they are: powerful obstacles to the grace of God. If, however, we want to know what a world not scarred by such barriers looks like, we need to look no further than St Paul's image of the early Church, a community that not only reflects the mind of Christ but which is also clothed in Christ and which finds, in Christ, no such barriers. 'There is no longer Jew or Greek, there is no longer slave or free, there is no longer male and female; for all of you are one in Christ Jesus' (Galatians 3.28).

Not The End

In the months during which I wrote this book, my father died. One of the things that most struck me about his dying and death was just how important the physical and material side of life became as the process progressed. As a priest I was used to holding the hands of the people needing support but was still surprised at how important touch was as he drew near to the end of his life and just how natural and instinctive it felt. Our relationship had never been very touchy-feely but it seemed right to hold and be held for long periods of time. A few weeks before he died I gave him a holding cross. He gripped it firmly and held it close for many a long hour.

In the early hours of the morning of his last night at home I sat next to him and held his hand. It was warm and soft. For most of his life his hands had been hard with the calluses made by using spanners and screwdrivers. For over 40 years they were engrained with the dirt of the engine oil, grease and grime of his trade. He was drifting in and out of sleep and so I thought my presence must be a comfort to him. In any case, I had much to meditate on that night. He was so disappointed that I had not followed him into the family business as he had his father. But that disappointment was as nothing to his disbelief when I said I felt called to be a priest. Yet over the years he developed a real respect for Christian ministry. Not, I think, because of the quality of what I did, but because of its openness to the pain of the world. He knew that there was something deeply right about being prepared to engage with life at its most raw and disorienting. For him, the valley of the shadow of death was a fearful place and he had a quiet respect for anyone who would share the journey of the dying or bereaved. This made it much easier than I thought it might be to be in touch with him towards the end. Like those celebrated in Jesus' beatitudes, he knew his need. But there are limits. At around 2.30 he opened his eyes and whispered 'Stephen! I wish you'd go to bed, boy.' So I did.

The next day he agreed to go to a hospice. In that setting, I noticed how all the family, who were gathering by the hour, would naturally offer a hand to be held as they took it in turns to sit with him in twos and threes. The excellent hospice staff attended to bodily needs in a practised and professional way, but it also seemed right for some of us family members to take our turn with the little swabs that would clear and moisten his mouth. On his last morning, we gathered in prayer around his bed, which was rolled into the little chapel, and I was able to anoint him. A few hours later, as he came to his last breaths, three generations of family squeezed as close to him as possible. Everyone wanted to be touching him or his bed or bedclothes or each other. Hands were squeezed and laid on in blessing. People also offered words of love appropriate for such a departure, but it was the touch that communicated most: do not go *lonely* into that good night. The day after his funeral, the same group stood in the hillside cemetery, his cremated remains having been placed in his own parents' grave. The brief prayers had all been said but it was not over until each of us took a small handful of the red Devon soil and crumbled it into the grave.

Reflecting on this six months later, I realized that this death is lodged in my memory alongside the births of both my children. I was quite startled to think this, but it really does connect. Being present at either threshold creates focused attention, heightened anxiety and intensity of action. Both create the sensation of being simultaneously at the edge *and* at the centre of life. Nothing else matters. And there is disbelief and wonder when breath has, in the one case, ended, and in the other, started. Birth and death are, perhaps, the most exalting and humbling of human experiences. Passion and humility interweave in both. Our human and Christian calling is to hold fast to them in the years between.

As Barefoot Disciples walking the way of passionate humility, we will sooner or later appreciate, like Job, that a truly spiritual path starts by learning how to be a *bodily* person. Indeed, you could say that learning how to be a person of clay who will one day become a small bucketful of dust is perhaps our major spiritual project. It is the project of learning true humility. The minor disciplines that we sometimes adopt in Lent can quickly alert us to this. They help us not only remember our mortality, but also to feel the strength of our own desires. If we think that giving things up is going to make us feel holy or spiritual, we are in for a surprise. Give up chocolate, and chocolate is what you will fancy. Give up beer, and you will feel like a wander down to the pub. Try fasting, and you will probably find yourself thinking about food more than ever. It seems absurd. The disciplines that make an impact on us seem to make us more carnal and less spiritual. This, however, is the point. We are human beings, not angels. We are Christians, not Gnostics. The animal nature remains part of us. Our real stuffing is but dust. For human beings, there is no spirituality which is not profoundly bodily. The time will come when our desires are transformed and our bodies transfigured, but there are no short cuts to holiness and the long route is always a pilgrimage of nature as much as of grace.

Ash Wednesday is the gateway into Lent, the season of bodily spirituality. It leads inexorably on to bodily death on Good Friday, which is itself the gateway into bodily resurrection which inaugurates another season of bodily spirituality. There is no getting away from it. Christian spirituality is bodily spirituality; for we are dust, and to dust we shall return. That is why we must turn from sin, which has its origins in the mind, and follow a person, not an idea. The Christ we follow is the Word who was made flesh to dwell among the children of Adam, the earthlings. We are people of dust, who share a planet and a fragile ecosystem with myriads of creatures, all made of the same unpromising material. Yet we are called to fullness of life as people of flesh and blood whose humility is only truly humility when it is both earthy and passionate.

One year, my wife and I decided to mark a special wedding anniversary with a small service of celebration and renewal of vows. It was a lovely occasion in the Galilee Chapel on a warm summer's afternoon. We chose as one of the lessons the story of the disciples on the road to Emmaus at Easter (Luke 24.13–35). The image of the couple out for a walk, talking about all their troubles and being joined by a mysterious companion, seemed wonderfully apt. As part of the preparation, I thought I would write a hymn for the occasion. One of the verses reflected the Emmaus road story:

When walking on the dusty road
We find your presence near;
And as you take and break and bless,
You cast out all our fear.

Our daughter was unable to attend the service, so I told her about the hymn over the phone. When I read her this verse, she said, 'Yes, like "Little Donkey".' At the time, I did not find the comparison very flattering. Until that point I had not noticed that I had quoted the famous Christmas song. But whether in a popular song or a hymn written to be sung just the once, or in countless biblical stories, the point is still the same: both the dust and the divine *matter*. The journey of life is both a place of dust *and* a place of divine encounter. When we have our feet on the ground, the loose and fragmentary surface on which we try to walk gets disturbed, and that, in turn, disturbs us. We get covered with its stuff. As we reach out to be in touch with others, we get our hands dirty. We cannot live without dirt any more than we can progress through life without approaching death. This is why God in Christ had his feet anointed. This is why God in Christ shows us how to wash one another's feet. This is why we have our heads marked with ash at the beginning of Lent and why, on Good Friday, Jesus is crucified barefoot and naked. It is why so many crucifixion scenes incorporate Adam's skull, the bones of his head. Dust and divinity are never to be separated in the Christian imagination, for they are reconciled in the flesh of Jesus Christ, the most human, and humble, of human beings. We must take off our shoes to follow him: for we are treading the holy ground of the real earth.

Notes

1. Wirzba, 'The Touch of Humility', p. 226.
2. Forster, *Howards End*, p. 188.
3. Sadgrove, 'A Christian Perspective on Being Human', p. 11.
4. Bede, *The Life of Cuthbert*, p. 69.
5. Wirzba, 'The Touch of Humility', p. 232.
6. Morisy, *Journeying Out*, p. 28.
7. Morisy, *Journeying Out*, p. 33.
8. Williams, *Writing in the Dust*.
9. Wilcox, *The English Poems of George Herbert*, p. xlii. The poems in question are, 'The Temper (1)' and 'Church-monuments'.

Bibliography

Adair, J., *Inspiring Leadership* (London: Thorogood, 2002).

Archbishop's Council, *Common Worship: Services and Prayers for the Church of England* (London: Church House Publishing, 2000).

Bede, *The Life of Cuthbert*, trans J. F. Webb in *The Age of Bede* (Harmondsworth: Penguin, 1983).

Benedict, *Rule of*, see de Waal.

Bennett, A., *Talking Heads* (London: BBC Books, 2007).

Bernard of Clairvaux, *The Steps of Humility and Pride*, trans Leclerq, J. and Rochais, H. (Rome: Cistercian Publications, 1973).

Book of Common Prayer, The (Cambridge: Cambridge University Press, n.d.).

Brueggemann, W., *The Prophetic Imagination* (Philadelphia: Fortress Press, 1983).

Casey, M., *Truthful Living: Saint Benedict's Teaching on Humility* (Leominster: Gracewing, 2001).

Collins, J., *Good to Great* (London: Random House, 2001).

Comte-Sponville, A., *Small Treatise on the Great Virtues* (London: Vintage, 2003).

de Waal, E., *A Life-Giving Way* (London: Continuum, 1995).

Dostoyevsky, F., *The Brothers Karamazov*, trans. David Magarshack (Harmondsworth: Penguin, 1982).

Dreyer, E. A., 'Humility', in P. Sheldrake (ed.), *The New SCM Dictionary of Christian Spirituality* (London: SCM Press, 2005).

Eliot, G., *Middlemarch* (London: Penguin, 1981).

Ford, D. F., *The Shape of Living* (London: Fount, 1997).

Ford, D. F., *Christian Wisdom* (Cambridge: Cambridge University Press, 2007).

Forster, E. M., *Howards End* (London: Penguin, 1989).

Francis, J., *Adults as Children* (Oxford: Peter Lang, 2006).

Harries, R., *Is There a Gospel for the Rich?* (London: Mowbray, 1992).

Herdt, J., *Putting on Virtue* (Chicago, University of Chicago Press, 2008).

Hershberger, M., *A Christian View of Hospitality* (Scottdale: Pennsylvania Herald Press, 1999).

Hume, B., 'A Cheerful Joyous Love', *The Tablet*, 16 February 2008, p. 15.

Hull, J. M., *What Prevents Christian Adults from Learning?* (London: SCM Press, 1985).

Hymns Ancient and Modern (New Standard) (Norwich: Hymns A&M Ltd., 1990).

Jamison, C., *Finding Sanctuary* (London: Phoenix, 2006).

Long, S., *Le Dossier* (London: John Murray, 2007).

McCabe, H., *God, Christ and Us* (London: Continuum, 2003).

McCall Smith, A., *The Right Attitude to Rain* (London: Abacus, 2007).

McCourt, F., *Angela's Ashes* (London: Flamingo, 1996).

MacIntyre, A., *After Virtue*, 2nd edition (London: Duckworth, 1987).

Mahaney, C. J., *Humility: True Greatness* (Colorado Springs: Co Multnomah Books, 2005).

Maxwell, J. C., *Failing Forward* (Nashville Tennessee: Thomas Nelson, 2000).

Morisy, A., *Beyond the Good Samaritan* (London: Mowbray, 1997).

Morisy, A., *Journeying Out: A New Approach to Christian Mission* (London: Continuum, 2004).

Murdoch, I., *The Sovereignty of Good* (London: Routledge and Kegan Paul, 1970).

New English Hymnal, The (Norwich: The Canterbury Press, 1986).

Owen, D., *The Hubris Syndrome* (London: Politico's, 2007).

Radcliffe, T., *What Is the Point of Being A Christian?* (London: Continuum, 2005).

Ramsey, A. M., *The Christian Priest Today* (London: SPCK, 1985 [1972]).

Ramsey, A. M., *God, Christ and the World* (London: SCM Press Ltd, 1969).

Roberts, R. C., *Spiritual Emotions* (Cambridge: Eerdmanns, 2007).

Sadgrove, M., 'A Christian Perspective on Being Human' in P. Subris, *Jane Alexander: On Being Human* (Durham: The Institute of Advanced Study, 2009).

Schopenhauer, A., *The Pessimist's Handbook: A Collection of Popular Essays*, trans. by T. Bailey Saunders, edited with an introduction by Hazel. E. Barnes (Lincoln: University of Nebraska Press, 1964).

Smyth, G., 'Brokenness, Forgiveness, Healing and Peace in Northern Ireland' in R. G. Helmick and R. L. Peterson, *Forgiveness and Reconciliation: Religion, Public Policy and Conflict Transformation* (Radnor PA: Templeton Foundation Press, 2002).

Taylor, B. B., *An Altar in the World* (Norwich: The Canterbury Press, 2009).

Taylor, G., *Pride, Shame and Guilt* (Oxford: Oxford University Press, 1985).

Valmiki, O., *Joothan: A Dalit's Life*, trans. by Arun Prabha Mukerjee (Kolkata: Mandira Sen, 2003).

Waite, T., *Taken on Trust* (London: Hodder and Stoughton, 1993).

Weil, S., *Waiting on God*, trans. by Emma Craufurd (London: Routledge and Kegan Paul, 1952).

Wells, S., *God's Companions* (Oxford: Blackwell, 2006).

Wilcox, H., *The English Poems of George Herbert* (Cambridge: Cambridge University Press, 2007).

Williams, R., *Writing in the Dust* (London: Hodder and Stoughton, 2002).

Wirzba, N., 'The Touch of Humility: An Invitation to Creatureliness', *Modern Theology* 24:2, April 2008.

Worthington, E. L., *Humility: The Quiet Virtue* (West Conshohocken, PA: Templeton Foundation Press, 2007).

Wright, T., *Matthew for Everyone, Part 2, Chapters 16–28* (London: SPCK, 2002).

Wright, T., *Virtue Reborn* (London: SPCK, 2010).

Acknowledgements

I should have realized early on that to try to write about humility would not only precipitate a wry smile in anyone I told, but would also be a significant spiritual journey. It certainly has been. My intellectual and formational debt to Rowan Williams was great before his invitation to write the book arrived. I have learnt so much in responding to it that it is greater still. That he embodies in his character so much more in terms of Christian virtue than I have been able to express here is just one reason why it is so easy to thank God for him.

I have referred quite extensively to my experiences on a sabbatical visit to South Africa in 2002. Thanking all those who helped me make those experiences worthwhile is impossible, but Andrew Wingate and Chris Burch in Leicester, and Jenny and Andrew Wilson, Edwin Arrison and John Oliver in Cape Town, opened the doors to many surprising adventures for me. That they were expecting me to write about forgiveness and reconciliation is another matter. Maybe that will come.

The debt that I owe to the good people of Loughborough is incomparable and runs through this book like letters through a stick of rock. For twelve years we travelled together on a journey which churchwarden David Johnson invariably described as a roller-coaster ride at the Annual Parochial Church Meeting.

It was often exhausting, sometimes exhilarating but, whatever else it was, for me it was a great learning experience.

I am eternally grateful to Maggie for so many things, but in particular for her patient support and wise guidance in this as in so much. Family life is a great educator – especially for parents. Rachel and James have given me so much in general but also in terms of this book. It was Rachel who got me to India and who was my companion on the train and bus journey in Chapter 8. What an adventure that was! James has put books and articles on my desk and been a great theological conversation partner.

Sharing drafts of parts of the book with people good enough to read and comment has been integral to its gestation. I have done so much of this that I fear that to attempt a list gives the impression that there is a limit to the help I have received. There is not. But among countless others, Anne Marsden, Andrew King, Ian Wallis, Robert Lawrance, Judy Hirst, Caroline Dick, Trish Thompson, Philip Crosfield, Anastasia Scruton, Jeff Astley, Dana Delap, Anne Lindsley, Judy Turner, Tom Wright and Maggie Cherry have been of significant help at different stages. Towards the end of the process Caroline Chartres at Continuum helped me to identify the weaker parts of the manuscript with great kindness and made positive suggestions with real tact.

Members of the Chapter and congregations of Durham Cathedral will recognize some of the ideas and stories in the book from my sermons. I am grateful for the wisdom and patience of many friends in that supportive and stimulating community, whose life of common prayer has provided the spiritual context for writing this book. Colleagues in the Diocese of Durham are always very patient with me, but I fear that I might have been more trying than usual while working on this project, so I am grateful not only for their encouragement, but also their forbearance. I am especially indebted to Joyce Parker for her steadfast and steadying professionalism at all times.

If we are serious about humility, sooner or later we will recognize that, however much we wander and age, we remain, in a deep sense, children. Extraordinarily, my parents met the Archbishop on his visit to Crediton not long after he so kindly asked me to write this book. Emboldened far beyond their norm, and encouraged by the vicar, they got past the photographers for a chat. My Dad was on the phone to me about it as soon as he got home. My heart was in my mouth imagining what he *might* have said. (He had already shared with me his view that I had plenty to do without writing a book, 'What, a whole book?') But he was bursting with pride and delight at the encounter. It is so sad that he died before the book was completed; but it is with deep gratitude and love that I dedicate it to my parents, Bill and Marie.